Lessons From the Forests

Lessons From the Forests

Ben Mathes with Laura Raines

WRITERS CLUB PRESS
San Jose New York Lincoln Shanghai

Lessons From the Forests

Writers Club Press
an imprint of iUniverse, Inc.

For information address:
iUniverse, Inc.
5220 S. 16th St., Suite 200
Lincoln, NE 68512
www.iuniverse.com

Ben Mathes with Laura Raines

ISBN: 0-595-23436-4

Printed in the United States of America

To my wife, Mickie, for her encouragement and constant support

To our sons, Benjamin and Adam, fellow explorers

And to our dogs; Alexander, for his wisdom, and Winston, for his loving companionship

I am blessed by you all, Ben

To Greg; my Mom and Dad; my daughters, Sarah and Frances; and my sister, Beth;

For saying, "Yes, you can!"

Thank you all for your love and encouragement, Laura

Explore the world and expand your universe.

—*Tamela Thomas*

Contents

Foreword

I was there at the very beginning of Rivers of the World, though I didn't know it at the time. I'm not even sure Ben knew. After eighteen years of traveling the world on behalf of international health development, he had taken some time off to rest and pray and consider a new call, but couldn't seem to shake a need to travel.

One day in the fall of 1994, I received the telephone call that changed my life. "Let's go to Africa," Ben said, as if it were the mall. By this time I was well situated in a comfortable and challenging suburban church and knew my place as a preacher, leader of committees, and director of staff. It was enough. And so I hedged. "Might I consider the next trip?" I asked. "I'd love to have you on that one, too!" Ben said, practicing his famous ability to convince. I signed on, but I was a reluctant convert.

Nine months later I was stepping out of a dugout canoe on the banks of the Sankuru River of Zaire, entering a village after dark, seeing the soft glow of their charcoal fires, hearing the children whispering our presence, sensing the movement of excitement gathering all around us. We were there to conduct a health survey and to inoculate the children against measles and polio.

For ten days, we had chugged down the Sankuru River in an old banana boat, hauling our supplies and medical equipment, cooking our own food, and slowly developing that legendary heart for Africa that so many others have discovered. There is so much pain there, and need. But the beauty of the place and the overwhelming humanity of it all have never left me. In fact, I have been back four times now, and I plan to go again.

Ben Mathes is a most remarkable person, and not just for his ability to inspire. He is remarkable for his heart and for the change he brings into people's lives. I am just one of those people, but through my experiences with ROW, others have been inspired to travel to Africa. Sometimes, I can't help but reflect on the unlikelihood of it all. Because of that telephone call years ago, my life and world have changed, and the little part of Africa we visit is fundamentally different.

When I was a child, one of the hymns we sang in church was "This World Is Not My Home." Maybe so. But because of Ben, it is a little more of my heart, and a little more of home than I would ever have thought.

Chris Price, Ph.D.

Preface

For almost a quarter of a century, I have traveled the world on behalf of one good cause or another. From international health development to plain old explorations, I have been blessed to learn so much from wonderful people in difficult circumstances.

As an American, part of my baggage has been the arrogance of prosperity that comes from living in this great land. I've seen the concept of the *ugly American*—who arrives on the scene with all the answers—played out ineffectively and harmfully, in too many desperate situations. In the travels I take and the stories I tell, I try to be guided by something that my parents pointed out long ago: *Every person considers his or her life to be just as important as you consider yours.* That's a pretty profound statement, when you think about it, and a powerful reminder when we're tempted to separate the world into *us* and *them*.

I'm grateful for the lessons taught to me by others. Prayerfully, they have impacted my ability to be a citizen of the world.

Acknowledgements

Happily, my life's path has crossed with Omba Ngandu, Shamba Akasa, Thomas and Sarai Ann Webb, Palmy Ventosilla, Max Walker, Marcel Telders, Chris Price, Beronica Infante, Papa Akula Munkanga, Will Powell, Buddy Mcrae, Faye Webster, Steve Schaefer, Ellen Grand, Ena Urbina, Roldan Rios, Nguyen Ha, Ray Davis, Lane Alderman, Britt Boyd, Adolphe Onusumba, Rick Justice, Preston Small, Linda and Mike Massey, Tamela Thomas, Jenny Merello, Papa Jon Haskell, Mike Reinsel, Molly Mednikow, Sam Wilson, Andrae Crouch, John Gallagher, Mike Millius, Spencer Millius, Henry Hurt, Molly Kinney, Van Kelsey, Lenny Stadler, Ed Lenane, Larry Nobles, John Lawrence, Emir Bashiri, Norman Plunkett, Mrs. Cleaver, David Klein, Hampden-Sydney College, Victor De Leon, and Judd Brannon. I remain humbled by your friendship and support.

Without Laura Raines, this project would never have happened. Laura is the very talented writer who brought these lessons to life. Thank you, Laura—you endured much from me—and did so gracefully!

And now, I commend these lessons to you. May you grow from reading and perhaps be reminded that every experience has a lesson to teach.

Beware the Dangers of Fast Food

Getting there was half the fun. We left a city called Bulape in a big truck, and we worked our way 50 miles north along the broken, rutted paths of the Congo interior to the village of Lodi. A truck had been pulled from the river. It had fallen from a capsized ferryboat and stayed under water for three months. In other places in the world, you'd have called the insurance company and gone out and bought a new truck, but this was Africa. Trucks weren't that easy to come by.

When we got word that the truck had been pulled from the river, we knew we had to act quickly. Once brought out of the water, it would begin to rust. It didn't look too promising, but we emptied all the fluids, added new ones, put in a new battery, and checked the tires to make sure they were okay. We climbed in with our fingers crossed, and, amazingly, the truck started. Not only that, it ran like clockwork. My friend, Chad, decided he would just drive the truck back to Bulape.

Now that I'd come all the way to Lodi, I thought it was time for a little adventure. Mother always said, "Be careful what you wish for, you might get it." But, as we all know, you don't become a big-time African explorer by listening to your mother. You become an African explorer by, well, exploring!

At the hospital in Bulape, I had recently photographed a hunter who had been lost in the forest and ended up with us. The missionaries were amazed that this man spoke a language they had not heard. At first I was astounded by this revelation, but in a

1

land of over 200 languages, this was to prove to be not all that uncommon. Still, I wanted to see if I could find this village.

Chief Bocongo, of Lodi, was willing to lend me two young boys from his village. We got in a dugout canoe and worked our way across the Sankuru River. Carried along by a swift current, we were going in search of the legendary Chief Ikongusamu of the DeKesee tribe in the village of Bulumbo. Once we got to the other side of the river, we caught some fish, burned 'em black and put 'em in our pockets. They'd make a great snack for later.

Into the jungle we went. The path couldn't have been more than two feet wide. The jungle was wet and dark and soon closed in all around us. We were barefooted. I had on shorts, a polo shirt, vest, and carried a camera with a long lens. I had one young man in front of me and one behind me serving as my guides. They spoke a language called Lingala. I can speak a little Tshiluba, but no Lingala. We couldn't communicate, so we passed the time by whistling. I sang some of my favorite songs. The boys would laugh at me, and I'd laugh at them. We were having a grand time, until the young man in front of me screamed for all he was worth.

Well, I'm a dad. I did what any dad would do. I snatched that little boy back and held him tight, and as I did, his companion jumped on my back and began screaming, too. Ahead of us on the path stood a man—a man with a bow and arrow who had drawn his bow and was aiming his arrow at the three of us. I would have screamed, too, but I was the adult in the crowd, so very slowly I put the first little boy down. Very slowly, I unwrapped the other little boy from my back. Just as slowly and deliberately, I raised my camera as if it were gun, pointed it at the man with the bow and arrow, and said, "Don't move!"

I could see the archer in the viewfinder of my camera. As he came into focus, I can distinctly remember thinking, this man's gonna shoot me, but I'm gonna get his picture!

My mind was racing. The man in front of me spoke yet another language, Otetela. Great! I've gotta deal with Lingala, Tshiluba and Otetela, when all I really wanted to do was meet Chief Ikongusamu.

Then it dawned on me. People who travel the river speak yet another language. They speak French. Slowly once again, I lowered my camera. I looked over the top of the zoom lens and asked, *"Voulez vous un foto?"* (Would you like a photograph?)

In an instant, the whole world changed. The archer transformed into a hunter before my eyes. Turning sideways, he struck a pose, raised his bow with a jaunty smile and said, "Ah, ha, ha, ha! Photo?"

I took his photograph. He went on his way hunting, and we went on our way to the village. By the time we arrived, the word was out—there was a white guy coming to visit! The whole village turned out, and they were lining the jungle path.

As I entered the village, I learned that the greeting was *M'bote.* That's Lingala for "Hi, ya'll." They said, *"M'bote,"* pointed at me and laughed. "Ha, ha, ha, ha, ha, *M'bote,* ha, ha, ha, ha, ha." Gee, that's just great, I thought, as I checked the zipper on my fly. I seemed to be the only one not in on the joke. They appeared friendly and since they spoke a language I couldn't speak, I decided to make the most of it. I walked through the village waving to everyone, speaking right out loud in English, saying, "Thank you, thank you, thank you. I'm so happy to be here. I wish my friends could see me now. It's just good to be here."

My plan worked. The crowd led me to Chief Ikongusamu, who looked to be about 70 years old. Chief stick in hand, he looked me up and down. I looked him up and down. Finally, he indicated that we should sit, and we squatted on the ground. He didn't have a lot to say, but it became apparent that we were going to share a meal.

A woman came by with a porcelain bowl and lowered it to the chief. He took a handful of whatever it was and tossed it in his mouth. I decided not to look, just grab a handful and toss it into my mouth. As I was releasing the bits of food into my mouth, I couldn't help but peek. They were smoked caterpillars. Now in case you were wondering, smoked caterpillars come in two types, with legs and without. These were with. They tasted like leather that had been held too close to the fire. But if you chew anything long enough, it will go away.

The dear woman came back, this time carrying a wicker basket. She lowered the basket to the chief. He put his hand in and fanned it back and forth as if cooling a piece of meat. He took something, threw it in his mouth and ate it. I decided it must be hot meat. It's sort of like eating chicken in public. Use a knife and fork if everybody else does. If they pick it up and gnaw, then just pick it up and hunker down.

I put my hand in the basket and began to fan back and forth, when I realized that it wasn't hot meat in that basket. The basket was filled with live termites. Now the termites were about two inches long and had big pinchers on them. The trick, as the chief demonstrated, was to bat your hand around, grab a bug, pitch him in your mouth, and bite him before he bites you. I figured I could do that. I grabbed a bug, tossed him in my mouth, and my very first thought was—thank goodness nobody speaks English in this village!

As you can imagine, I was jumping up and down, trying to bite the bug and trying not to yell, because the bug was clearly winning. He was trying his best to eat his way through me, while I was trying to bite him! The chief thought this was hilarious and the dear woman who was serving me got very concerned. She reached into the basket. She pulled out a bug, smushed it on her hand, then wiped it on my hand. I had to scrape it off with my teeth.

I made two mistakes. Mistake # 1 was eating the bug in the first place. Mistake # 2 was looking up at the woman and saying, *"M'balu bimpe,"* a combination of languages that means, "That's pretty good." She got an assembly line going—pluck, smush, wipe, scrape; pluck, smush, wipe scrape; pluck, smush, wipe, scrape. I ate bugs 'til I thought I was gonna pop.

While I made a friend of Chief Ikongusamu, the downside of the story is that there's very little soap in this part of the world. Neither the woman's nor my hands were very clean. Bless her heart. Whatever grew on this woman's hands, and mine, grew in my stomach. I ended up sick with what must have been a combination of things: cholera, diphtheria, typhoid, tetanus, break-back fever, backwater fever, dengue fever. I must have had every disease known to man. I lay in my bed thinking, this is it. Guess mom was right. Dr. Walt Hull from the hospital walked in, stood over me and said, "Mathes, you can die anywhere you want to. I don't care. But you're not gonna die on me. It'll look bad. So, get outta Africa."

With that, he air-shipped me to Brussels to live or die. Sabena Airlines and the Metropole Hotel cared for me. Zaire, as it was called at the time, had been a Belgian colony, and they were experienced at receiving the ill from the heart of Africa. I am grateful for their generous and gentle care to this day!

Well, I'm here, so I must have survived, and the point of this story is very obvious. Please—in your own life—never, never eat smushed bugs off the hands of a stranger.

Weathering the Storm

Do you remember when a horrendous tidal wave devastated the small country of Bangladesh? In a matter of hours, 168,000 people died. That's more people than I can comprehend.

It wasn't until months later that we finally got word from the people who lived in the southern part of this country and began to hear their stories. Let me start by saying that Bangladesh is on the Indian subcontinent, and that it is the delta of all the rivers of the old Soviet Union and China. Streams come together to form the Ganges and the Brahmaputra rivers in what is one of the rainiest countries on earth.

The country is perfectly flat. When you look at the horizon it is straight ahead. During the monsoon season, one moment the sky is bright and blue. The next moment, you see a gray line on the horizon, and then you know you're in for it. It is as if a thick, gray blanket dropped down over your head. You're gonna get wet. That's all there is to it!

The first fellow who wrote to me was a farmer. He had no idea that the storm was coming. He, literally, looked up and saw the tidal wave crashing across the land in front of him. The only thing he had time to do was to climb onto the roof of his house in an attempt to get above the flood and survive the storm. The air was filled with blowing debris. The man was knocked unconscious. When he came to, he was still on the roof of his house, but his roof had blown five miles away from the rest of his farm. That's the kind of power we're talking about.

Another man was also a farmer. He was a farmer, but more importantly, he was a husband and father. This man had a wife and five little girls. He also owned a radio, which meant that he had the privilege of knowing in advance that all he loved and owned was soon to be destroyed, and there wasn't a thing he could do about. Or was there?

You have probably seen the clothing that women wear in this part of the world. It is called a sari. It is the traditional outfit and consists of eight to ten yards of cloth. The women drape it over their shoulder and wrap it around them. It's a very attractive costume.

In the face of the worst storm of his life, this man did the only thing he knew to do. He took the cloth from his wife's sari, and he cut it into long strips. Then, one child at a time, he took his little girls and climbed to the top of a coconut tree. He tied them to the tree to ride out the storm.

When I read his letter, I couldn't help but wonder. What did he say to them? Was it something like: the wind will blow, the rain will come, hold fast to the tree, and you'll be okay? Here—I'll put your sister up here with you. So maybe there are two little girls in this tree. Then he goes over and ties two more in another tree. He takes his wife and baby and ties them into the top of a third tree. And, finally, when all of the members of his family are fastened to the top of coconut trees, he takes the cloth that's left over, climbs to the top of a tree, and he ties himself there.

Again! What was this man thinking? If one of my children dies, who could I live without and ever be the same? If something happens to my wife, who will look after us? If something happens to me, who will look after them?

The worst storms always seem to come at night, don't they?

In your life, have there been times when you've done everything you can do and you still have to let go? It's not easy to be a parent, even under normal circumstances. You do everything you can to raise your children right, to keep them safe, and then you send them off to school. You walk that child into the first grade classroom and with forced cheerfulness you say, "This is Miss Sally. She's going to be your teacher. This will be so much fun. I'll see you after school." Then you walk out into the hallway and break down and cry.

Have you ever put everything you had into a business and had it fall apart? Did you try your best in a relationship, but just couldn't make it work? Did you sit beside a hospital bed and hold a hand you've held most of your life, and then at some point had to let go? Life is full of small and large storms.

The storms in Bangladesh never come as a few drops. One moment you're surrounded by a thick darkness that is so thick you can feel it. The next you hear a rumble in the heavens and then the sky collapses. The rain comes so hard you have to cover your head. Just like the storms in our lives, these storms finally go by. The sun does come out the next day.

For this man, the sun came out indeed! As he dug himself out from under his wet clothing, he looked around and saw that all he owned, his home and all his crops had been destroyed, but his wife—his wife and all five of his children—had survived the worst storm of their lives.

Resolve in your mind today: to hold someone you love, to write the letter you've been meaning to write, to make that phone call, to affirm someone before once again the storms of life come rolling in.

And when your own storms hit, remember to do the best you can with the resources you have; then let go, trusting that at some point, the sun will come out again.

Gone Fishin'; Got Caught!

I didn't really steal the Bronco. I just borrowed it. I had been in Zaire for almost ten days. I'd been with the same people, in the same setting, at the same hospital, and it was time to finally get away and do something for myself.

You've been there. It's sorta like having company in your own home. I mean you can get too much of people after a certain point, and I decided—well, first trip to Africa and all—I could find the river, and I would go fishing. Seemed like a good idea to me.

I got in the old Ford Bronco, you know the square kind that can go almost anywhere, and I left Tshikaji on the one road that headed out of town. I just *knew* that it would eventually intersect with the river, and I'd do me some good African fishing.

I had visions in my mind of two types of fish, one called *n'dimbo*, which is as big as I am (and that's big), and the other called *putu*. *Putu* has razor sharp teeth and is about the size of a frying pan. I could just see myself fighting those fish, playing out the line, then reeling it in, and when they got good and tired—why I'd just pull 'em out, one after another. I'd use my Swiss Army knife to gut 'em and bring 'em back for my friends at the hospital. They were going to be so surprised and pleased that I was a successful African fisherman.

I drove off in the sunrise with visions of African animals—elephants, zebras, horned creatures of the Great Plains—but all I found was elephant grass and a few mud-hut villages and some termite hills. Most of the animals of the Congo are long gone. They were eaten for protein when trade routes disappeared due to bad government, wars, and neglect. You might see the occasional chicken or goat, but not much else.

Time sorta drags by when you're driving down an African dirt road. Every kilometer of jungle foliage looks pretty much like the kilometer before it. And—although I hate to admit it—after several hours of creeping along, I still hadn't seen any sign of the river. I thought it had to be around here somewhere. I passed some more termite hills, and then the road disappeared in a patch of elephant grass that reached almost as high as the Bronco. Believe me, you can't see anything submerged in a sea of elephant grass. I was relieved to finally come out the other side, and then the road forked. Don't you hate it when that happens?

Well, the right fork looked like it was dipping down. I figured the river must be down low, so I dipped down. Into the woods I went. The trees closed in to swallow me. Time dragged by some more. I realized I was lost. If I had to turn around and drive back toward Tshikaji, I'd have no earthly idea how to do it.

A passenger got in the car with me. His name was Doubt. And Doubt reared his ugly head and said, "Uh huh! Thought you could just travel across Africa, didn't you? Figured you'd go fishing and have a big time. Now you're lost! They'll never find you, Mathes. Or if anyone finds you, it will be one of those tribes who like to tie people to sticks, rip 'em in half, and fling 'em in the air." As you can see, Doubt had seen his share of old Tarzan movies.

Finally, a clearing appeared miraculously on my right. Ah, civilization at last. The clearing sported a rectangular, thatched-roof hut with open sides. Logs had been split in half and turned over to form seats. Hanging from a nearby tree was the metal wheel from a truck. On the ground below it was a crowbar. It looked like a bell, so I picked up the crowbar, pulled back for all I was worth, hit the wheel, and it gonged through the jungle. It sounded so good; I thought I'd do it again. That way, I didn't feel so alone. I pulled the crowbar back and hit that metal wheel again. It gonged through the jungle—and the bushes came to life.

People started flooding into the clearing and surrounding me. This was my first time to the Congo, and I was surrounded by a sea of faces all speaking a language I didn't speak. I did what many of you would do. I got back in the car and shut the door. Doubt and I stared at the growing sea of faces outside the window, feeling more or less safe, until someone opened the passenger-side door. Someone else opened my door. He put a hand in, took my arm, and gently led me from the truck.

Now some people are struck dumb in a tense situation, but that's never been my approach to crisis. When in doubt (or with Doubt in this case), I always say talk fast and gesture broadly. I held my hands up and smiled to show what a friendly, lovable guy I was. "'Scuse me...ha ha ha..." I laughed. "I'm just passing through. No really. This is nothing big. No reason to panic. I'm just heading down to the river to go fishing. Didn't mean to bother anybody."

But wait a minute. Two people had climbed into the truck. "What are you doing? Don't get in the truck. It's not my truck," I protested. They opened the glove compartment. "Why are you opening the glove compartment?" I yelled. Now, someone was opening the back of the truck. They began pulling out the floor mats and pushing the seat forward to look underneath. They were gonna strip this truck right in front of me, and there was nothing I could do about it, I thought. Doubt was in full agreement, but he wasn't saying anything, so I decided to give it another try.

"Uh...'scuse me," I said loudly. "This is not *my* truck," and I pointed to myself for emphasis. "The truck belongs to the hospital. Really, don't strip the truck. I mean I'm just borrowing it, and—hey, does anybody speak English here? I'm just curious...any English-speaking people in the crowd?"

"Excuse me."

What was that? Did somebody speak English?

"I said, 'excuse me,'" a voice in the crowd answered.

"Oh, thank goodness! Thank goodness!" I couldn't believe it. "Yes. Who speaks English?" I called again.

"Well, I speak English," said a man stepping forward.

The man explained to me that his name was Kidane. He was a teacher in the village, and as he spoke, my whole life changed.

"Please, don't you have a book or a magazine, something we could read?" he asked. "We know the truck comes from the hospital. They always bring us something to read. We have three, maybe, four books in our village. My friends are so hungry for knowledge that they tear the pages out of the book, and they go back to their homes and memorize what it says. Then they bring it back and swap it for the next page. Please! Don't you have anything we can read?"

Books? Magazines? Who would have thought? In my mind, I had been afraid that they were going to strip the truck. I had brought a lot of baggage with me on this trip: a couple of changes of clothes, video and camera equipment, some gifts for the people serving overseas, writing utensils, two pairs of shoes…things like that. But I also packed some unseen baggage with me—baggage I brought from one country and carried to another. Because I was lost in a strange neighborhood, I assumed that these people were going to steal the truck. It never crossed my mind that they might be simply looking for something to read.

Not Forgotten

The Caribbean region of the world is often plagued by horrible hurricanes. Water and high winds often ravage the remote islands, tossing people, animals, trees, and shelters about like so much confetti. For people who already live in abject poverty, hurricanes only make things worse.

While I was working in Haiti, one such hurricane made its aimless and wandering trek across the island. Without rhyme or reason, it totally destroyed some areas, while leaving others virtually untouched. In the wake of the storm, we were left to pick up where we had left off.

Not knowing where to start, we fell back on routine and decided to travel to the village of Fayette, which was normally about an hour's drive from our base of operations in Leogane. Not, however, in the wake of a hurricane.

It took us over eight hours to reach Fayette, and the road was strewn with unbelievable sights. Dead animals lay on either side of the dirt path, swollen and bloated from drowning, left to rot in the sun. The stench was overpowering. At one stretch, we passed a graveyard where coffins had erupted from the graves and been tossed about helter-skelter. Huts had been swept away; garden plots lay buried under mud. Sometimes we had to stop and lift a fallen tree blocking the track. Other times we stopped to assist people or to answer questions about other villages. All about us was destruction and despair—the despair of people who had lost what little they had, and hadn't yet summoned the energy to go on. We were tempted to turn back. Why travel to a remote part of the island when there was so much work to be done close at hand? Still, something made us press on.

When we arrived in Fayette, our worst fears were realized. Our clinic building, like most of the village, had been destroyed by the hurricane. Amazingly, the people of the village had gathered around the remains of the building and were waiting patiently for us.

You see it was Saturday—our usual day to hold clinic in Fayette—and they were waiting. Living in a remote village without electricity or telephone, they had no idea whether we were alive or dead. For all they knew, the entire rest of the island (or the world) might have been swept into the sea. Yet, they kept their faith.

Even though a hurricane had destroyed their village, they believed that the people who said that they cared about them would be there on Saturday, as usual. They believed that we would show up on the appointed day, and by the grace of God, we had.

When I'm tempted to believe that the little we do can't matter much in such a hurting world, I see again the joy in those villagers' faces and remember. It's not just medicines and vitamins that we bring to people living in remote areas. It's the hope that comes of knowing that they're not forgotten. A loving presence can make all the difference.

Avoid Old Friends Bearing Bananas!

Because we make do without many of the comforts we are used to in America—electricity, hot running water, TV and fast food restaurants—people who listen to our stories might get the impression that working in a developing country is always difficult, depressing, and hard. That's just not the case. A lot of times it is so exciting and surprising that it just completely catches you off guard. Let me give you a good example.

I was working in the northern part of Thailand in a wonderful facility called the McKean Rehabilitation Hospital in Chiang Mai. Our job was to refurbish some of the homes near the hospital so that patients who were handicapped, burned, or suffering from a trauma would have a place to live while they healed and adjusted to life.

Late one afternoon, I was sitting in the lobby of the Downtown Inn in Chiang Mai. I was minding my own business, reading a newspaper, when I looked up and in walked Bob and Betsy. Now Bob and Betsy live in Nebraska. What were they doing in Thailand? "We found you! We found you!" they kept yelling as they made their way across the lobby.

They had traveled all over northern Thailand purposely looking for me, and at last they had me in their sights. We hugged and laughed, and they shared with me their reason for the search. They had come all the way from Nebraska to get married. Specifically, they wanted me to marry them in Thailand. I told them I didn't know if I could. I advised them to go talk to officials at the

American Embassy and in the Thai government. If it was legal and possible, then it was fine by me. After they left, I sat shaking my head that two old friends had shown up in Thailand and tracked me down.

The next morning they were back with all sorts of paperwork. We signed everything appropriately and announced that the wedding would take place that very afternoon. We gathered all of our friends. At the appointed time, Bob and Betsy showed up in a van filled with 400 pounds of bananas. They had hired a local driver named Poo to drive to the wedding site. I didn't ask any questions. I just piled in and figured that this was going to be one of my more interesting weddings.

Away we went. We drove through the northern jungles of Thailand along the Mae Winn River. We came to a beautiful clearing, and Poo stopped the van. We climbed out, and I figured we were gonna eat some bananas, which seemed suitable for a jungle wedding. I looked across the river to see four elephants lumbering down the side of the mountain. They swam the river and came right up to us. Guess what? Each elephant received a hundred pounds of bananas as a snack. After they'd polished off the fruit, Bob and Betsy announced that we were going to have a wedding on the back of these elephants.

Well, I'd ridden elephants before. I figured I could do it again. We hung flowers all over the elephants, and decorated everybody as well as we could. Bob and Betsy climbed up into a seat, and I said, "I guess I'll just follow you on the next elephant." Then the surprise!

"No, you get to drive the elephant and lead the wedding party," said Betsy.

She was beaming at me, glowing in the way that brides do. Even though I thought I was too big to sit on the head of an elephant, I guessed I could give it a try. As I gingerly climbed up on the elephant, my friends hastened to assure me.

"Don't worry!" Bob said. "The guide will put a leash on the elephant's ear. He'll just lead us around like a pony ride, and then we'll get married."

The skin of an elephant is like sandpaper. The small hairs are like wire bristles rising from the shoulders of the beast. But a pony ride didn't sound like such a big deal. It sounded okay.

The guide walked over with his leash. He flipped it towards the elephant's ear. The elephant jerked his head to the side. The leash fell to the ground, and the elephant headed towards the river with me holding on for dear life. The very tender skin of my thighs was scratched with every step. Ouch!! Not wanting to dampen the nuptial mood, I raised my hand above my head, waved it around in a circle and cried, "Hi ho, Silver! A—way!"

We crossed the river. We climbed the mountain. I was still clinging to the beast and trying my best to make it funny. Apparently I succeeded. Bob and Betsy thought our situation was a scream.

Two hours later, we were on the other side of the mountain. I pivoted on the head of our elephant and married Bob and Betsy, while our friends sang songs in the background. Having pulled off this remarkable feat, I thought it was time to go home. That's when Bob and Betsy sprang on me another Thai tradition. They announced that *now* my job was to pole them down the Mae Winn River and get them back to town.

A bamboo raft appeared. Someone handed me a 30-foot piece of bamboo. Bob and Betsy placed themselves in the middle of the raft in marital bliss and left me to pole them down the river. What no one told me was that this river was really nothing more than a series of rapids cascading down a mountain, and the bamboo pole was to keep us from crashing into the rocks. We rambled along for six miles until we finally docked at Chiang Mai. "Is it time to go home yet?" I inquired hopefully.

"Oh no! Now we're all going to dinner to celebrate the wedding," was Betsy's ready reply. She seemed refreshed and exhilarated after our river trip. What's a guy to do?

We climbed back into the van. Care to guess who drove us back to town? Who else? The couple had chosen a very special restaurant. It was dark when we got there. The owner greeted us very formally and announced that we were going to have quite a celebration. He handed me another bamboo stick. Tradition, be hanged, I thought. I ain't poling anybody anywhere else today! Instead, he led me to a dark pit. He instructed me to put the stick into it and wave it around. Must be magic, I thought. I waved it around, and the pit came to life with an ominous hissing sound.

The pit was filled with cobras and pythons! We were given the rare opportunity of choosing either a cobra or a python from the pit. I chose a cobra, and the staff went to work. They tied its mouth shut. They split the snake open and drained the blood out of the poor reptile. They mixed the blood with gin, and gave it to me to start our meal.

I looked at the waiter and said, "Thank you, no. I had my snake at the hotel earlier in the day—and one snake a day is all I'm good for!"

When it was all said and done, half of us dined on fried cobra for dinner, while the other half enjoyed a rack of python ribs. Let me just say that working in out-of-the-way places in this world is exciting and challenging. Sometimes, it is also frightening and humorous. Never would I have guessed that two old friends from Nebraska could have created such a marathon (and memorable) adventure in Thailand.

Now you may be wondering what lesson to take away from this story, so let me move right to the point. If you are ever in a situation where you are offered cobra or python for dinner, and it could happen—the world is a smaller and stranger place than you think—let me suggest, always go with the cobra.

Adventures and Coconuts

By definition, an adventure is a daring enterprise—an unusual and exciting experience with some risk involved. We know that when we head down a river, there are no guarantees of happy endings. This is life, not a fairy tale. All we can do is take each bend as it presents itself.

On one of our South American adventures, our ship left port before we arrived in country. The good ship *Tucanare* left Iquitos and worked its way across the Amazon to the Yavari River, the natural border between Peru and Brazil. Heading south, our plans were to send the ship down an offshoot of the Yavari and join it on a remote expedition.

When we arrived in Iquitos, we learned that the Peruvian air force was going to fly us over the jungle to locate our ship. What an amazing experience. Our floatplane took off on the river and flew low over the water. Our eyes were peeled for the *Tucanare*. When we spotted her, the plane set us down in the water, and we transferred our supplies to the ship.

Our team had decided to head for the Galves River in southeastern Peru. We wanted to meet the famous Cat People, or *Mayoruni*. This tribe considers itself descended from the jaguar, and they tattoo their faces to resemble the large cat. We traveled the Galves River for three days without seeing a village or a human being. Even in remote jungle areas, this is highly unusual. We did see a variety of anteaters, macaws, some monkeys and lots of caiman. The captain began reporting that the river was dropping. There hadn't been enough rain, and if the river got too low, we could be stranded in the middle of the jungle.

We decided to press on, when we were hit with a totally unexpected calamity. At one bend in the river, we were attacked by a swarm of insects that we couldn't even see. We soon felt the result of the encounter, however. Each bug left a bite on our necks and arms that our corpsman told us had to be cut open in order to kill the eggs that had been laid under the skin. Some of us had several hundred of these bites and treating them was a really nasty business. They itched, and we looked like we'd been infected by the plague.

We finally located the village of the *Mayoruni* and began to try to introduce ourselves. We had brought mosquito nets to give them, because this part of Peru is caught in a malaria epidemic. Mosquito nets are one way to cut down on the number of mosquito bites, which spread the disease.

We noticed that only mothers and children came to greet us at the first village. Some of the women's faces had been tattooed with the teeth of the jaguar. Their bottom lips were pierced and had bamboo sticks inserted to represent whiskers. Their noses were also pierced and sprouted bamboo whiskers on either side. In the second village, only children came out to greet us, and by the third, we realized that we had seen very few adult males.

Through our interpreters, we learned that the men had taken their bows and arrows into the woods and were deciding whether or not to attack us. These were not friendly people, and since our guiding principal is always to work *with* people to help them solve their own problems, there was nothing we could do. We had reached a dead end and were forced to turn back.

Fortunately, ROW does not encounter many closed doors. For many years, our teams have served with the Yagua people on the Napo River. Each summer we have provided educational supplies for their children, dehydrated soup to make them strong enough to take malaria medicine, basic health care, and eyeglasses. Even now we are raising money to equip a hospital ship that would serve the medical needs of almost 147,000 people who live along the Napo River.

What is most needed in this part of the world, though, is relief from the malaria epidemic. The malaria parasite is transmitted from person to person by the bite of *Anopheles* mosquitoes. The bite can cause anything from a moderately severe infection to a highly fatal illness, depending on the type of parasite and the person's physical condition. Mosquitoes breed in the fish ponds that are located near villages, and while pesticides will kill the insects, the chemicals are costly and damage the environment.

While documenting health conditions of villages around Iquitos, ROW learned of a natural mosquito-larvae fighting bacterium called *Bti* (*Bacillus thuringiensis* var. *israelensis*). Harmless to people and other animals, *Bti* kills the larvae of black flies, which spread river blindness, and *Anopheles* mosquitoes, which cause malaria. When we learned that a Peruvian scientist was studying the possibility of growing *Bti* in a coconut, we recognized an open door for ROW.

Think about it—coconuts! Something that grows naturally in the jungle, and is free for the taking once it drops to the ground, could be a solution to one of the most serious health risks in the world. Seizing the opportunity, ROW funded, staffed, and equipped a laboratory at the Institute of Tropical Medicine at the University of Peru six years ago. Our Peruvian scientists; Palmira Ventosilla, Beronica Infante and Jenny Merrello, working with ROW scientist, Max Weber, discovered that *Bti* introduced into a coconut via a cotton swab would live and grow. Left to incubate for 90 hours, the coconut could then be cracked open and the pieces thrown into a mosquito-infested pond. In field tests, Ventosilla found that *Bti* lived in the water up to 18 days, virtually killed all the mosquito larvae in the water, and controlled their further growth for up to 45 days.

ROW teams have been distributing *Bti* kits to remote villages, where they teach people how to grow the bacteria in coconuts and throw the pieces into their ponds as one way to reduce malaria. Draining standing water, cutting back weeds, distributing mosquito nets, and continuing to educate people about the disease are also part of the program.

Ventosilla tells us that the *Bti* project will never fully eradicate malaria from Peru. It's impossible to control the problem in all of the jungle. But by consistently using the *Bti* kits and coconuts, villages can control their own ponds—and that's enough.

When we can find ways to help people take control and improve their lives, it's more than enough!

Grief is the Same in Any Language

It was late in the afternoon. The day was done, and it was time to relax and head down to the river to take a bath. Now we use a place that's called the Chutes, because the water moves very rapidly there. The idea is that hippos and crocodiles don't like fast-moving water; you can get in, take a bath and get out again without becoming somebody's lunch.

We were in the old truck heading down a long, dusty dirt road. And I guess it was 50 or 60 yards ahead of me, I saw someone rolling across the dirt road. I could tell it was a woman, and I could tell that she was very old. It occurred to me that maybe she was having some sort of a seizure or a convulsion. I sped the truck up, and as I started to get out, someone waved me off. A young man explained that there had been a death in the woman's family. This dear woman was simply grieving in a very expressive way. As I watched her anguished movement, I said what I guess most of us would say, "I'm so sorry. I wish there was something I could do." And I drove on.

I got the better part of a mile down the road when I just had to stop the truck. I looked at my friends and said, "I can't leave that woman lying in the dirt. I've gotta go back."

And they looked at me and said, "Mathes, what are you gonna do? Your French is embarrassing. Your Tshiluba is just awful. What do you think you can do?"

"I don't know, but I'm not gonna leave that lady in the dirt."

As I turned the truck around and headed back in her direction, I was thinking as fast as I could. Well, what was I going to do? I knew nothing of her background or beliefs. There are many Christians in Africa but also many who believe in witchcraft, voodoo, animism, and other things. What if my attempts to help only scared her? I hadn't really settled the issue by the time I got back to her. She was still in the dirt. I decided the least I could do was tell her about me. I knelt beside her, put my hands on her shoulder and said, *"Jesu Udi Mukelenge"*(Jesus is Lord). I figured at least I could say that much. As soon as I did, she quit crying. She wiped her eyes and stood up. She took my hand, and we started walking down the dirt road together.

My friends followed me at a distance in the truck and later told me that we looked like two old friends out taking a stroll. I spoke right out loud in English, "Now Lord, I can't speak this lady's language, so you interpret for me." I held a hand at shoulder height and said, "You know I've got two little boys. I've got my Benjamin, who's right here, and then, I've got my Adam, who's right here," and I lowered my hand to his height. She looked at me and somehow seemed to understand. She raised a hand to her shoulder and talked awhile. Then she lowered it a bit and spoke again. She lowered it a little more and said something else. When she got way down low and tried to talk, she just collapsed on my shoulder and started to cry.

A man came from the village and explained to me that it was her grandson who had died. The boy was four years old and had starved to death. He wasn't in the ground yet and this woman wanted to know if I would come and just be with her family. How could I not? We walked on through the elephant grass until we came to the typical village of mud huts with thatched roofs.

As we came closer to her house, I could hear family members crying and wailing. They pulled the curtain aside. I lowered myself and climbed into this very dark and very cold mud hut. The fire had been pushed to the side. In its place there was a little mat, and upon the mat lay the body of this little four-year-old boy. His hair was gray. His skin was dry and wrinkled. His belly was bloated. He was wearing his best clothes, and his arms were crossed over his chest.

I sat on the floor with the family, and we held hands and rocked back and forth. There were no words I could offer that they would understand, but it didn't matter. Grief is the same in any language. After awhile there really wasn't anything else to do. I asked if I could come back the next day and help bury the child.

In the meantime, I returned to my room and lay down on my bed. I felt the things I've felt too many times before and since. I felt big and fat. I felt sick to my stomach. Malnutrition, one of Africa's greatest problems, was no longer an impersonal diagnosis for me. Right then it carried the face of a four-year-old, little boy. I could understand why a grandparent would be reduced to rolling in the dirt. There seemed to be no reason on earth why that boy should die when I—who had seen it all and done it all—should be living so well. I couldn't escape the question; why did that little boy have to die? As I was feeling the pain that dealing with senseless hunger always brings, someone started singing outside my window. I thought, oh great! Here comes company, just what I need.

When I got up from the bed and pulled aside the curtains, you'll never guess what I saw. It was a little girl. She was the size of an American four or five-year-old child, so I imagined she was six or seven years old. She was baldheaded. See, when children are malnourished their hair turns gray or red or brown, and sometimes parents think that if they shave the child's head, it will be okay. This child didn't have any hair. She was barefooted and her dress was tattered, but she was skipping in my front yard, and she was singing.

Right then, that child looked like an angel, and I couldn't help but smile. You see, she was one of the children from our nutrition center. Called, *Tudisha Bana Bimpe* in Tshiluba, it means "place of good eating." Caring people from other parts of the world had fed her with the food she needed to grow strong and healthy. No, we didn't get to the little boy in time. The little boy died, but this little girl we had reached before it was too late, and she was going to be just fine.

When I saw the little girl and heard her singing and then thought of the lifeless body of the little boy—I saw clearly the choice and opportunity that life offers us, if we'll only stop, turn back, and take a closer look. We can lose ourselves in grief and despair—throw up our hands and back away, because we don't know how to start solving the overwhelming problem of hunger on this earth. Or we can act in the hope that more of the world's children will be full—full of food and energy and joy.

Because we had chanced on the uncontrollable grief of one boy's grandmother and understood it without words, we knew where and how to act in this case. We were able to send in nutritionists, doctors, and nurses. We could supply food and agricultural knowledge. It was the kind of help that would see that no one had to starve in that village again.

The world is a big place with so many problems, but if we all just started where we saw a need, think what we could accomplish.

The Road to Lodja

"I'm not sure how much more of this boring, luxury travel I can take. Maybe I'll try an adventure safari next time," said Buddy. It was a valiant attempt to bring a little humor to our situation, and it failed miserably. No one even smiled.

Well, it was hardly the time for stand-up comedy. It stood to reason that a crowd of exhausted, worried, white-knuckled guys, hanging on for dear life to the back of a pickup truck as it raced through a war-torn jungle, would make for a lousy audience. The man wasn't thinking clearly. But I'm getting ahead of my story. Let me tell you how Buddy and the rest of our ROW team got into this predicament.

The Congo was caught in the middle of a terrible civil war. Just two years before, Uganda, Rwanda, and the Banyamulenge tribe had helped put President Laurent Desire Kabila into power. Now united as *Rassemblement Congolais pour la Democratie* under 36-year-old, President Onusumba Yemba Adolphe, many of the same forces were fighting for freedom from the dictator, Laurent. Wars in the Congo have been fought over the rich mineral resources in the Kasai Province, tribal conflicts, corrupt governments, and failed economies. The result is always more suffering for the people of this region.

So despite the war, ROW continued to deliver medicines and immunizations to remote villages, until the war came too close. Fighting along the Sankuru River, the Army of the Congo confiscated our ship, the *Kuto Misa*, and took hostage our staff members, Omba, Shamba, and Papa Akula. They forced our staff to pilot military arms and soldiers up and down the river instead of delivering medicines to the villages. We found that totally unacceptable.

We began working with the Army of Uganda to see if we could get into the country to free our friends. Fortunately, after three months, our men escaped, and Shamba, our ship captain, managed to sink the *Kuto Misa* right out from under the Army of the Congo. We were elated! Our intrepid Congo staff had triumphed without our help, but when the first flush of victory passed, we knew that nothing had really changed. People were still suffering from river blindness and dying of tuberculosis, polio, measles, and malnutrition. Too many Congo children would never see their fifth birthday. Our staff had no ship and no supplies. We knew we had to go back.

And we knew it was going to be a challenge. With our normal routes cut off, we had to fly to Kigali, Rwanda, to get into the Congo. There, we negotiated with Russians to fly us in a Russian cargo plane into the middle of the war. I had $60,000 in cash in my backpack and a half pound of gold Krugerands in a leather belt around my waist—just in case. We negotiated a price and time of departure. We filled the Russian Antonov 32 with medicine, equipment, and supplies bound for our base in Lusambo in the Kasai Province.

As the Antonov landed in the dirt and slid along the runway to a stop, we saw hundreds of rebel soldiers who were not sure who we were or what we were doing in their part of the world. Thank goodness, local leaders greeted us with hugs. We watched as the soldiers relaxed and lowered their weapons.

We off-loaded all our equipment and supplies and traveled seven kilometers into the village. We were allowed to set up headquarters in an abandoned convent. For a few days, part of our staff negotiated with government leaders and discussed health needs, while the rest of us attempted to stage a music video. Never let it be said that a ROW trip is not interesting! Seven-time Grammy Award winner, Andrae Crouch, had written a song for ROW to make people aware of our work in the Congo, and we wanted to film it on location (as they say in Hollywood). Mama Mboomboo organized the village into a lively rendition of "I want to see you when you smile!" You've never seen such dancing!

With the video "in the can" and permission to work granted, we piled into a 40-foot-long dugout canoe. Rwandan soldiers, guerilla soldiers, and Dr. Onusumba would be along for the ride. Our plans were to travel 100 miles down the Sankuru River, offering healthcare clinics and hope to people in the remote villages.

The trip was exhausting. When not crammed into the canoe, we were either hiking through the jungle, working in the villages, or setting up camp on sandbars. Even if we met with no rebel soldiers, there were still hippos, crocodiles, and snakes to think about. At our first campsite, as the soldiers were being assigned tents, Dr. Onusumba asked, "Where am I going to sleep? I have no tent."

"That's okay, you can sleep with me," I said.

He looked at me with this strange expression and said, "But you're white!" We all laughed so hard we cried.

"Yep," I answered. "You might as well get used to it. Just get in the tent and go to sleep."

Dr. Onusumba and I became very dear friends, and I can tell you from first hand experience that he snores worse than I do.

At the end of our journey we reached the village of Bena Dibele. A truck was supposed to be waiting for us but after lugging all our gear to the top of the hill, we learned that the truck had broken down in the jungle across the river. We were trapped…in the Congo…in the middle of a war!

Exhausted and with no ready solution at hand, we sat down to share a meal of goat with the rebel garrison commanders. As we talked about our work, I remembered that I was carrying ROW bracelets with me. They're dark green and have our website, **www.row.org**, embroidered on them. I gave some to the rebel leaders, and they put them on immediately. The color matched the green in their camouflage suits. I could tell that they thought they looked pretty good. Never again will I underestimate the power of fashion, because the commander's attitude changed dramatically.

"I have a truck, and I have decided that you can use it to escape this war," he said suddenly.

We still had to travel 100 miles through the bush through enemy lines before dark, but we had wheels—we were excited. We were a little less excited when, after piling our gear into the back of a Land Rover Defender 90 pickup truck, we had to force our legs down between the baggage. It wasn't just uncomfortable. If the truck flipped, we were not going to be able to jump free. We had already made the decision to make as much noise as possible as we traveled, so that enemy soldiers would think we were an ordinary supply truck and ignore us until we had passed.

As the gravity of our situation set in, I asked our chaplain, Dr. Chris Price, to say a prayer before we set off. As I bowed my head, I noticed that he was holding an AK-47 machine gun. That image of Chris will always stay on my heart.

The truck took off, and we immediately realized that we were going to be bounced to pieces with only the side of the truck to sit on. The road was almost non-existent—the jungle perfect for an ambush. Things were tense to say the least, and Buddy's comedy routine had fizzled, so I figured it was my turn. In an attempt to lighten the mood, I dug into my suitcase and pulled out a small video camera.

"Hey guys, I've got an idea. Let's turn on this video camera and everybody say goodbye to their families. That way if we're killed, maybe somebody will find the camera and our loved ones will know we were thinking about them."

I thought this would cheer everybody up—it didn't. We turned on the camera, and the first time we passed it around everyone was as macho as he could be. The second time around, people took it a little more seriously. I put the camera away, wishing I hadn't brought it out.

We bounced along in silence for another hour or two and I had to speak up again. "Hey, guys, do you know what I do when I'm scared? I sing. And the more scared I am, the louder I sing, and I always sing the same song. Would you like to hear it?"

They all told me NO, but I told them I'd sing it anyway and began, "I wish I was in the land of cotton. Old times there are not forgotten. Look away, look away, look away, Dixieland," and I proceeded to sing all of "Dixie."

Now I want you to try and imagine a truck full of Americans, Rwandan and rebel soldiers zooming through a war in the Congo singing, "...look away, Dixieland," at the top of their lungs. We all laughed and it helped us feel better, for a while.

At one point we stopped to stretch our legs, and the driver told us that we had to cross six bridges. All of the bridges had been blown up. The good news was that all of them had been rebuilt; the bad news was that they had been rebuilt out of bamboo. I don't know about you, but where I come from people use bamboo to catch fish. I knew this was going to be how we would die.

The driver decided that if he hit the bridge really fast, we should weigh less and we'd be okay. Seemed logical to us—that tells you what shape we were in—but it worked! It was the most frightening experience of the trip, but we crossed all six bridges—and then what little road there was disappeared entirely.

As it hit ruts the size of the Grand Canyon, the truck would rear up on two wheels with us hanging on for dear life. As we hit a particularly bad bump, Buddy, our resident comedian, screamed at the top of his lungs. All of us figured he had either lost his mind or broken a bone. We hit another bump and he screamed again, but this time he also yelled, "Is that all you've got? Then give me some more!"

Before we knew it, we were all chanting and clapping with each bump, "Is that all you've got? Then give us some more!"

When we finally made it to Lodja (our destination), we had no food for two days. We had to filter water into our canteens from small puddles in the road. We managed to wheedle our way onto a Russian flight, even though they weren't expecting us at all.

We had made our way into the Congo, re-established our ROW operations, and made it back out. We were safe, and we had learned a lot about fear.

The first thing we did on the return trip was to say our prayers. If you're afraid, do the same. It's the best way to face a tough situation. Then we made a video for our families. Let me remind you that in times of fear, you may feel like you're by yourself, but you're not alone. There are people who care about you. They can help if you just let them know what you need. If you are alone, think of people you love or admire and draw strength from them.

We sang a song. My favorite spirit-lifting song is "Dixie." What song do you sing? If you don't have a song, get one! You never know when you may need it. When the fear still wouldn't go away, Buddy looked it straight in the eye and yelled, "Is that all you've got? Then give me some more!" It didn't decrease the danger, but it sure made us feel better.

We did those things and it carried us through one of the most frightening experiences of our lives. I hope you'll remember them when your life gets frightening.

Free Speech?

You know, I don't really care if I was set up or not. I will never in my life forget what happened while I was visiting hospitals in the cities of Chongju, Kwangju and Sunch'on, all on the peninsula of southern Korea. I saw wonderful facilities staffed by even more wonderful people. One of the joys of being a visitor in what seems to be the most polite and proper country left in the world is that, as a visitor, *you* are treated as the most important person of the day.

While touring a 16-story hospital with thousands of employees and 800 beds, I had to go first. It didn't matter that I may never have been in that hospital. I had to lead the parade. So there I was out in front. Behind me came the medical directors, the administrators, the chiefs of the different departments, the residents, the interns, and the nursing staff. We were quite an entourage working our way through the hospital in Kwangju, Korea.

I had been in Korea long enough to acquire a wonderful Korean name. It's *Majatsu*. It has something to do with being a smart horse in water, but that's really all I know.

As we toured the Kwangju hospital and were heading toward the basement, the staff began to whisper among themselves. They were getting excited about a particular surprise they had in store for me. I had no idea what it could be, but the anticipation was growing. I really wanted to hurry a little bit, because I was excited to see what they had in store, and the tour had been kind of formal and dry, to be honest with you.

We worked our way down to the basement, and I walked into a room that had a glass window, not unlike the glass window that separates you from the teller at the drive-through window of a bank. I looked through the window and sitting in the room was one nurse and a little boy. The little boy had his hand on the throat of the nurse. He had his other hand on his own throat, and with a very solemn intensity, was obviously practicing something very important. Dr. Ha, the medical director, shared with me that this little boy could neither hear nor speak, and that he had been practicing with all his might to do something very important this very day.

We tapped on the glass and the nurse, who was actually a speech pathologist, turned her head and smiled. She brought out the little boy who was almost shaking with excitement at our meeting. As he walked into the room, we all fell silent. Clearly, it was show time, and he had center stage. That young man put his hands to his side, drew himself up, took a deep breath, and with the greatest determination he could muster said, "*Anyung-hashimeka, Majatsu,*" and then he bowed.

He rose back up with tears streaming down his face. The pathologist started to cry; the medical director started to cry; I started to cry, and we all three threw our arms around this young marvel, who with the greatest effort had managed to say, "Good morning, Smart Horse in Water!" What a wonderful surprise. I don't know that I've ever heard more beautiful words in all my day. It was humbling. That child, who could neither hear nor talk, had worked so hard to simply greet me.

I can't help but wonder what it would be like if we had to work just as hard to form every word. I wonder what things we would say, but I wonder what things we would leave unsaid as well.

Family Behavior

I guess we all want to share the things we do and love with our children. For me, that's getting to know different people in different places in the world and finding ways to help them solve their problems. So when my son, Benjamin, was 18-years old, I took him with me to the Chiapas region of southern Mexico. Had I known more about the situation, I might have opted for a different country, but you know what they say about hindsight.

The Zapatista guerillas had been waging a war against the government of Mexico on behalf of the indigenous people in the region. Long ignored by mainstream politicians, their demands included better roads, a hospital, and a university to educate their people.

Irma Garcia de le Torre, a Presbyterian missionary and friend, met us in country. We planned to travel the Chiapas region together looking for opportunities of service. Our first stop was a town called Okosingo, south of Mexico City, where Irma had family. They had a harrowing tale to tell.

In a recent battle, the guerrilla forces and the federal forces had engaged each other in fighting in the middle of the town square. The police station had been shot to pieces and many people killed. Irma's family worked in an office building on the square. High enough to be relatively safe from the gunfire, they watched the sudden battle unfold before their eyes. Even from that distance, it was a terrifying experience.

During a lull in the battle, they managed to escape the building and make their way back home. There they hid for three days, praying for the safety of their family and friends. Provisions ran low as the battle continued, but a woman who worked for the family volunteered to find food. In spite of the battle, Maria slipped out of the house and returned with two large grocery sacks filled with staples and canned goods. How had she managed it, they wanted to know? She had broken into the grocery store and stolen what the family needed. When the battle was over, she would go back and pay for the groceries. Irma's family was touched and amazed that she would risk her life to help them. To Maria's mind, the choice had been simple. She had known them so long that she considered them family. When your family is hungry, you feed them. Anyone would have done the same, she said.

When we left Okosingo, Irma, Benjamin, and I traveled to an area called Aquazul (Blue River). We wanted to hike up the mountain following the river and see what people's lives were like in the jungle. The Blue River is absolutely breathtaking. The river comes crashing down out of the mountains, and it is bright, very clear, clean and cold. The mountains are covered with lush jungle foliage and everywhere there are birds and animals—so many sights and sounds to delight the senses. At the foot of the mountain is a large pool where people come to bathe and wash their clothes.

We left our truck at the bottom of the mountain and started climbing the path beside the river. As we got further into the jungle, the people we met all told us the same thing.

"You shouldn't be hiking here. You need to go back. This is not an area for you."

We didn't listen, but kept going. The higher up the mountain we went, the fewer natives we saw along the way, but those we did meet were even more adamant in their warnings.

"This is not a place for you! Rebel forces control this area, and you should not be here. Turn around and go back!"

This happened several times, but the warnings didn't daunt Irma. She finally told us why. "Did you know I was born about three miles farther up this trail? I bathed in this river until I was 16 years old. Would you like to see where I was born?" she asked.

Benjamin was 18 years old and had never been in a war zone before, and I wasn't sure how he felt about continuing. I asked him if he wanted to keep going, and he said, "Sure!" Ah, the confidence of youth!

I said, "Benjamin, here are the rules. You will stay behind me. If we run into somebody, you're not to say a word. You're not to make eye contact, and you're not to move. Do you understand that?"

"Yes, Daddy," he answered.

"Okay, let's go."

We started climbing, and the trail rapidly grew more challenging. We had to cross over one of those swinging bridges—you know the kind you see in jungle movies that transverse a deep ravine and seem to be hanging on by one worn thread. This one wasn't very long, but it was long enough to swing back and forth and bounce up and down. I've never been fond of swinging bridges, but Benjamin was behind me, so I forged ahead as if it was no big deal.

No sooner had we crossed the bridge than the trail plunged into a big cornfield. The corn grew high on either side. We were walking along cautiously—when right in front of us—a six-foot-long, black snake slithered over the trail, passing from one cornfield to the other. Now I may have mentioned before—I DON'T LIKE SNAKES! In fact—I CAN'T STAND SNAKES! But Benjamin was there, so I took a deep breath, regained my composure, and hiked on.

We were wearing boots and backpacks and carrying lots of media equipment. Past the cornfield, the trail grew rocky and we had to climb over some boulders and work our way through the jungle without banging ourselves, or our equipment, into the rocks. It was hot, all-consuming work. One of the easiest traps to fall into when out on the trail is not paying attention to the environment around you. I will confess that I was more concerned with not tripping over something or banging my knee on a stump than I was with what was going on around us. I hadn't realized that we were no longer alone, until two men stepped out onto the jungle path right in front of us.

We all jumped. It's frightening to be suddenly confronted with strangers and not know what is going to happen, but I stood my ground. Benjamin stood his behind me, and Irma began to speak.

"All of this land used to belong to my grandfather. As a child I bathed in this river. My home was right on the other side of the rise."

The guerrilla soldier looked at Irma closely, handed her his walking stick, and placed his hands on her shoulders. He said, "I used to work for your grandfather. It's okay. You are safe. You are with family."

The tension dissolved, and we all hiked a little farther up the river to see where the Aquazul first bubbles up out of the rocks. It was breathtaking, and we enjoyed a peaceful afternoon visiting with the soldiers, talking, and taking pictures. It could have turned out very differently, however. Later, once the demands for better roads, a hospital and a university had been met, the Zapatistas decided that it wasn't enough. Angry over former injustices and feeling pretty powerful, they decided to reclaim their former ancestral lands by force. They kicked legitimate landowners off their farms and burned their homes. There was more fighting, bloodshed, and heartbreak. It was hard to believe that this was the same group who had been so friendly to us on the mountain. They had shown us a much better side of themselves—because Irma was family!

Have you noticed that we all behave differently when we're around those we hold dear? Maria willingly risked her life to bring food to her family. I've realized that I'm braver when I'm on the trail with my sons. I'm thinking more of their safety and comfort than my own, because, well, I'm the Dad. I love them, and I want to protect them. Even guerrilla soldiers in the middle of a war were willing to set aside their suspicions and treat us with hospitality, because of the special relationship they had with Irma. Can you imagine how different the world would be if we remembered that we all belong to the same family—and treated each other accordingly?

Bill's Amazing African Adventure

Bill knew *who* he was and *what* he was called to do. Bill was a missionary. He lived in Africa and he traveled from village to village, pillar to post, sharing his faith.

It never crossed his mind to wonder what else he could be doing with his life, because Bill believed he was where he was meant to be. When someone is that sure of his vocation, it doesn't make life easy or predictable. It doesn't save him from danger, hardship, or loss. But it does make it easier to navigate when life takes an unexpected turn into uncharted territory.

Bill told me one of the most amazing stories I'd ever heard, as I changed his tire one day in the African jungle. You see, the tire on the Toyota Land Cruiser blew out while we were heading down a dirt road toward one of Bill's villages. Someone had to change it. I was younger, so the job fell to me, but Bill made me a deal. While I changed the tire, he would tell me a story I'd never forget.

Bill had been born in Africa, raised in Africa, and spent his whole ministry in this part of the forest. He knew the land and its people well. On this particular day, Bill and a friend had been on the road for about two weeks. They were dead-tired, but they were also like horses heading back to the barn spurred on by thoughts of home. They were zooming through the forest, when Bill came around a turn and slammed on the brakes. A tree had fallen across the road. Getting out of the truck, Bill was thinking that they could put chains on the tree, pull it out of the way, and keep going. Then he noticed that someone was sitting quietly on the tree.

The tree hadn't just fallen, the young man explained. The men from his village had placed it across the road as a warning. Just past the tree, the bridge had been washed away. If Bill had kept going, he might have driven straight into the river. While he was grateful to have escaped an accident, his hopes sank as his guide explained the proposed detour. He listened carefully, knowing that there would be no bright orange cones or road signs along the way.

In order for them to make it back to their village, they needed to turn the truck around. They had to head back into the forest, take the first three roads to the left, the second two to the right, get to the river and talk the ferry boat captain into giving them the extra diesel fuel they would need for the rest of their journey. Then they had to take the boat across the river, come up the back way by Mushinge, and work their way back up to Bulape. Sixty miles!!

That meant that driving through the forest at a brisk three, maybe four miles an hour, it would take Bill and his buddy most of the night to get to the river. Once they got there, they'd have to wait for the ferryboat. If the man took them across and shared diesel fuel, it would be almost suppertime the next afternoon before they got home. With no other options, Bill turned the truck around and headed off into the African sunset.

Hours dragged by. The darkness fell.

There are no lights in the jungle at night. Campfires are extinguished early. People go to their homes and pull the rags across the opening. They're afraid of the dark, so they stay inside.

You don't really visit when you drive through the jungle. The roads are bad or non-existent. They are so filled with ruts that it takes all you can do just to hang on. You know you're lucky to have any kind of transportation—you would never expect to find the latest model, the correct parts, or luxury items, like shocks, in this part of the world. So you bounce along trying to keep the truck on the road and yourself in the seat. Then there's the smell. Jungle vehicles are diesels, so they smell like a truck stop. In the rainy season, many of the roads become impassable. In the dry season, you ride with the windows rolled up because the dust comes flying in, and it gets in your eyes, your nose, and your teeth. Are you getting a picture here?

Bill said that it got toward midnight, and he realized that he was in a part of the forest that he'd never been in before—when all of a sudden, his headlight shone on someone standing in the middle of the dirt road. Dumbfounded, he stopped the truck. Standing in front of him was the tallest African woman he had ever seen. Her hands were outstretched, and she was wearing a white robe that fell to the ground. Every bit of exposed skin was painted white. Before Bill could say anything to his companion, others wearing white robes and white body paint surrounded the truck.

They opened the truck doors, pulling Bill out one side and his friend out the other, then prodded them both into the forest. As they were pushed along, they could hear the sounds of drums pounding. As they got closer to the sounds of drums, they could smell smoke. Torches had been dipped in diesel fuel and set on fire. The air was thick with the acrid smoke. It burned their eyes and their nostrils as they were pushed closer and closer. They came to a clearing in the forest. In the midst of the clearing, there was a tall stake rising straight into the air. Around the stake were torches burned brightly.

"Bill, what did you do?" I asked. "I'd have taken off for the truck by this time, hoping my buddy was a fast sprinter, cause I wasn't waiting..."

But Bill didn't run. He knew he was in Africa for a purpose, and his faith had never let him down before. He also knew that, sometimes, a detour might be an opportunity. So as the drums pounded, the torches burned, and a crowd in their dress whites pressed inward, he waited. Suddenly, the drums stopped. The tall woman who had met him on the road stepped forward, looked him right in the eye and spoke.

"We knew that you were coming tonight."

For a minute, Bill stood speechless. "You couldn't have known," he finally sputtered. "I'm only here because a bridge washed away many hours behind me. I have no idea where I am, and you could not know that I was coming tonight."

Unfazed, she told him, "We serve the unknown God, and He told us that you were coming tonight to tell us His name. Tell us. Who is the unknown God?"

Now Bill could have argued. He could have asked a lot of questions. He could have tried to figure out how they might have found out that a missionary would be traveling through their neck of the woods in the middle of the night, but he didn't.

"So what did you do?" I asked, impatiently, for Bill had fallen silent and seemed lost back in thought.

"Well, Ben, what else could I do?" he said with a grin, "I told them!"

"As he handed me the lug nuts, and I tightened them, I thought about Bill's story and his dedication. Life doesn't always run smooth. Certainly, Bill's didn't. I should know; I had just changed his tire!

We are all going to face complications and frustrations along the way. But if you know who you are and what you're supposed to do, you'll be a lot less likely to be sidetracked by life's detours.

Christmas in Bangladesh

My friend, Dr. Patti, ran a clinic in a place called Aladipuhr. It's in the Rajbari District of one of the most wonderful countries in the world, Bangladesh. To immunize 500 children against the terrible and unnecessary disease called polio was her latest challenge. She preferred to use the injectable vaccine, because it's a little more stable, a little less likely to spoil, in the less than perfect conditions of a remote area. It takes three injections to get the job done, to make sure that a little girl or boy will be immune from polio.

Dr. Patti was in the middle of a series of shots when her refrigerator broke down. She lost 500 doses of vaccine. Five hundred children were at risk from this stupid disease. It was Christmas time back home in the states, but Dr. Patti didn't care what season it was. She was in Bangladesh with a problem. Children were at risk. So she sent me a telegram. It said quite simply, "Mathes. Need 500 doses of polio vaccine. I need it NOW. Patti June."

My first thought was, well, that's just great, just where I want to be for Christmas time…sunny Bangladesh. Scrooge-like I grumbled and groused for a while. Does she have any idea how hard it is to travel during the holidays? The airports will be jammed. What about my family's plans? I can do the "Bah, humbug" bit as well as the next guy, but the thought of those kids…well, I did the same thing you would have done.

I went to the local drug store and asked the pharmacist to order 500 doses of polio vaccine. I knew it had to stay cold, so I went to a store and bought an ice chest. I bought those blue things that you freeze to keep food cold for picnics. I picked up the vaccine. I froze the blue things. I had my ice chest. I got tickets to Bangladesh. I was good to go!

I realized that there was a lot of room left over in the ice chest. Now I could have exchanged it for a smaller chest, but that's when the spirit of the season caught up with me. It was Christmas time, after all. I went to the local grocery store and bought the biggest, frozen Butterball turkey I could find. I put it in the ice chest and packed the polio vaccine all around it. I added the blue things and taped the chest shut.

Before I could leave, other telegrams appeared at my door. Missionaries had heard that I was coming—everyone wondered if, perhaps, I could just bring one small gift for each child, some needed bandages, syringes, batteries, maybe a little candy, …

I went on a shopping spree. Watches, batteries, candies, toys, socks, and underwear piled on top of catheters, syringes and boxes of 4 x 4-inch gauze. I had two large boxes of gauze, two cases of syringes, two footlockers of gifts, an ice chest full of polio vaccines—and a turkey!

I checked my luggage in the Atlanta airport. It flew in the belly of planes from Atlanta to London to Bombay to Calcutta to Dhaka. As we entered Bengali airspace, we were given customs forms that listed all the things we could not bring into this Islamic nation—batteries, toys, watches, candy…and my heart sank! I had the entire *forbidden* list with me. What could I do? I envisioned myself spending the rest of my life in some dreadful Bengali prison reserved for smugglers of toys!!

The scene in the Dhaka airport was beyond description. It seemed that every flight landed at the same instant. Hundreds of visitors were piling inordinate amounts of luggage onto four-wheeled carts and trying to get through customs. A glass wall separated us from our families and friends. As I waded through the mob, I found and commandeered a cart. Amazingly, every piece of my luggage had arrived. I loaded it onto the cart and glanced up at the glass wall. Dr. Herb Coddington saw me as I saw him. Our eyes met. At first he was overjoyed to see me. But as he looked at the amount of stuff on my cart, his expression collapsed, and I got scared. He shook his head and walked away. I supposed he had written me off as so much customs bait. I had to act!

I put my hand on each piece of luggage and prayed. I told the Almighty that the children deserved the toys just as much as Dr. Patti needed the medical supplies—HELP!

I scanned the customs area for just the right opportunity. A soldier seemed to stand out by himself. I pushed the cart through the crowd, tossed the gauze in his direction and yelled, "You can help me!" The gauze actually hit him in the chest. I thought for a moment that perhaps I'd overdone it. But the gauze was light. The box bounced off his chest, hit the ground, and made a great first impression.

"What do you want?" the startled officer asked.

"Well, I have to get through customs. My friends are waiting for me and *you* can help me."

"What do you have here?"

"Oh, this is a box of gauze for the doctor." I smiled, confidently, as if this explained everything.

"You must open it."

"Oh, if I open it, I'll get gauze everywhere." I stood my ground and stared at my new friend.

"Okay." He set the box behind him! I tossed another box of gauze his way.

"This is just more gauze," I said, and he placed that box behind him. I was on a roll! I set a crate of syringes in front of him.

"And what is this?"

"Why these are syringes."

"You must open them. I must see."

"But if I open this, I'll get syringes all over the place." He stared again, and with barely an audible sound, muttered, "okay," and moved the box behind the counter.

He accepted the second box of syringes without question, as I lifted the first footlocker onto the counter. I explained that it was full of medical supplies and gifts for the missionaries. He explained that he *had* to look inside.

This was it—prison time!! I unlocked the locks and slowly opened the box. Catheters were stacked on top of the toys and batteries and watches.

He lifted a catheter, and I explained its use. He shuddered, set it back, and closed the chest. I almost fainted!

When I set the next footlocker before him, he said, "I *must* look in here."

"Awww, you'll get medical supplies and catheters all over the place…" Seeing his face, I added, "Well, maybe just a peek…"

I, literally, undid the locks, opened the latches, lifted the top, showed my friend a *peek,* and slammed it shut before he could react! His eyes told me I'd better do something quick. I plopped my backpack on the counter.

"You better look in here," I said. It was filled with my personal effects and clothes. He rummaged for a bit, zipped the backpack shut, and set it behind him alongside the second footlocker.

I looked up, and out of the corner of my eye, I could see the missionaries and Dr. Coddington cheering me on. I was not alone and it felt good! All that was left was the ice chest with the polio vaccine—and the turkey! I gently placed it before him.

"And what is this last piece?"

"It's full of polio vaccine." No, I did *not* tell him about the turkey—I confess that to you now.

"I must look inside."

"You don't want to do that. We'll get polio vaccine all over the place." I stared at him for the last time. I held my breath.

"Okay, you may go," he said finally. He placed the chest behind him. I gathered up the cart, said my thanks and began leaving. My friends were jumping up and down and hugging each other. I was home free!!

As I was about to leave for good, I heard a voice call after me rather strongly, "Wait a minute!"

Slowly, I turned—

"I want to ask you something."

"Yes?"

"Why do you do this? Why do you bring this and come to my country?" My mind was racing for an answer. It arrived in time.

"For God."

"For God?"

"Yeah, you know, Allah."

"Allah—thank you—you may go."

I pushed my way past the last of the officers and into the arms of my friends. We cheered and some cried. Christmas had come to Bangladesh! We distributed the toys and batteries and watches and candies and took the vaccine out into the forest of Bangladesh, and guess what?

We got to immunize 500 children against polio, and we got to share a Butterball turkey. Now that's a Christmas dinner to remember!

Friends, it's not hard to change the world. It isn't impossible to make a difference somewhere else on this globe. You simply have to do it! Make up your mind that you can make a difference today.

Finally, many thanks, to that long-forgotten customs officer in the Dhaka airport. You could have made my life very difficult. I suppose you knew that something *wrong* must have been in those cases at Christmas-time, but you let me pass. You accepted my "We'll get stuff all over the place!" explanation as reasonable and let me go. Because of you, we had a celebration, and 500 children were spared the ravages of a stupid disease. Bless you.

Soldiering in El Salvador

Most people think of fighting, guns, and bombs when they hear of our armed forces stationed overseas. It's true that a soldier's first mission is to fight for our country and freedom, but there's often more to it than that, as I learned first hand.

During the war in El Salvador, I had a chance to visit and travel with some of our Special Forces advisors. Their job was to make daily forays to remote villages to conduct civic activities. The military uses these relief efforts to lift the hearts and minds of people caught in war.

Each day we flew to the villages in Huey helicopters. The fellows who fly these birds are amazing. Young pilots, and younger machine gunners, would climb aboard and help strap me into the seat. We had been advised to watch for white puffs as we flew over the jungle. That would mean rockets, and if we saw any we were told to keep our eyes open and be ready to respond quickly. Comforting words! I can so vividly remember trying to act like I did this sort of thing all the time.

On my first incursion into the war, I went on patrol with local citizen militia members. Armed with rusty WWII .30-caliber carbines, they must have looked a bit foolish to the rebel soldiers, who had the best weapons Castro could send. The guardhouse that offered the militia a base had recently been attacked by a rocket propelled grenade. A three-foot hole had been blown in the side of the shack. One man's arm was badly mangled. We replaced his bandage, arranged for his transport to the hospital, and headed out on patrol.

Patrol conversation consisted of the guy in command giving lessons to the soldiers and me. Colonel Pete was kind enough to try and point out ways to "sense" the presence of the plastic *minas* (land mines) used to disrupt life. Each step was precarious, but again—I tried to act like I did this all the time!

We flew to a village called Lamajada. Colonel Pete and I had a chance to visit with local political leaders and interested citizens. While we talked, the civic activities team quickly set up a clinic and began treating people who were sick. There was no way to know if the patients were pro-guerilla or pro-government, but they were all sick. The purpose was to show compassion to people who were trapped in the middle of this devastating war.

When the clinic was over, a truck appeared carrying bags of corn donated by the United States. The soldiers handed a bag to each family to help nourish them during this difficult time. In any guerilla war, one of the first things lost is the ability for poor people to tend their crops. During the fighting, crops are burned, fields are destroyed, and farmers are often too frightened to till the land.

After the bags of corn were handed out, uniformed El Salvador and US soldiers carried out the final civic activity for the day. They asked parents to bring their children to the town square, where they would receive free haircuts. A small service, and certainly not a crucial one, you might think, but there was an important reason for it. By giving the children haircuts, talking and smiling with them, touching them in a friendly way, the soldiers had a chance to show the kids that they were people, too. They weren't always engaged in the act of killing people. Not long before in this region, rebel forces had stood 40 people up against the wall and machine-gunned them to death. The bullet-pocked wall still stands in that village.

On this particular circuit, we made our way to several forts, where I saw other U.S. Special Forces soldiers advising the Army of El Salvador, as they pursued humanitarian activities. One young soldier told me that he was trying to care for 250 children who had difficult cases of bronchitis, flu, and upper respiratory infections. He needed my help. Could I possibly find medicine and send it to him in El Salvador, so that he could treat the children? I told him that I would do my best and left the country more impressed than ever by the professionals in our armed forces. These guys weren't just concerned with weapons or battles. Some were concerned about the health and well-being of children caught in a war zone.

I visited several hospitals in my effort to understand the war. In one hospital there were over 600 soldiers who had stepped on land mines and were missing one or more limbs. I took photographs of each of those men and sent the pictures back to Mrs. Inez Duarte, the first lady of El Salvador, who presented them to the men.

Sadly, land mines don't discriminate between adult soldiers and innocent young civilians. At the Benjamin Bloom Children's Hospital, I saw children who had stepped on land mines and were healing from burns or missing limbs. Some of the patients had lost their entire families to land mines. There lives were changed forever. But many would recover physically, thanks to the care they were receiving.

I came back from El Salvador excited and thankful for a broader definition of soldiering. Not long after I returned, I read a newspaper article about the war that mentioned the death of a young soldier at a remote fort. He had been killed in action, and the columnist was using his death to support his position of wanting the U.S. out of this (or any) war. As I read closer, I realized that the soldier in question was the same man who had asked me for medicine to help the children.

Outraged to see such a fine young man's death used in that way, I wrote an editorial to the Atlanta newspaper, in which I told the story of my visit with the young soldier. It made no sense to use his death as fodder in the war against the war. I wanted readers to know of the gallantry and compassion of this young man. His concern for 250 children had left an indelible mark on my heart. The *Atlanta Journal-Constitution* printed my editorial, and I didn't think much more about it until a few weeks later.

The phone rang one day and I picked it up to find the family of the young soldier on the other end of the line. They asked if I was the one who had written the editorial about their son. Someone had sent them a copy, and they wanted to tell me how much it had meant to them. It felt good to know that my words had done his family some good, but the story doesn't end there.

Before another week had gone by, the phone rang again. Someone on the other end of the line asked abruptly, "Are you the guy who wrote the article about the soldier in El Salvador?" Here it comes, I thought, someone's bent out of shape about what I wrote. Still, I assured him that I was the author of the article. Imagine my surprise when all he said was, "Well, good. Buy the medicine it takes to make those kids okay. Let me know how much it is and where to send the money."

As I worked out the details of our young soldier's request with this charitable stranger, I thought, we never know how or when we are going to touch someone else's life and make a difference. This young man had impressed me so deeply, that after his death, I couldn't help but write about his definition of what it meant to be a U.S. soldier and citizen of the world. Now I knew that—one last time—the soldier had answered the call to duty and inspired a response. It made me proud to have known him.

African Nights

There's not a lot to do on a sandbar in the middle of a river in Africa once the sun goes down. It gets dark about 6:00 p.m. in the Congo. The Sankuru River basin is right on the equator, and darkness falls like a curtain. One minute it's nice and light, and the next it's dark. There's very little twilight in the jungle.

It doesn't matter. Most nights, we are tired after a long day of working in a village, setting up camp, and finding water. All we want to do is bathe quickly in the Sankuru River and eat dinner. We wash and shampoo with an eye peeled for hungry wildlife, while struggling not to be carried away in the swift current. We climb back onto the sandbar, dry off, and put on the clothes that we'll wear for the next day or two—or even three. It doesn't matter. We're not concerned with fashion in the Congo, and we don't have to worry about color coordination either. We know that everything we wash in the river comes out the same rich shade of light mud.

Once everyone is clean, Papa Akula, our *chef de expedition*, calls us over for dinner. It's either rice and beans and greens, or it's beans and rice and greens, but sometimes, it's greens and rice and beans. We put some bottled hot sauce on it to add a little variety. It's really very good. Papa cooks the best rice and beans in all Africa!

There's no TV or radio, so once the meal is over, many people just go to bed. Others go to their tents for a while to read or be alone. Our days are busy so a little space is good for the soul. If someone builds a campfire, though, we all tend to gather around it. What is it about campfires that inspire stories?

Papa Akula leads us off with words that sound like, "Shamoo, shamoo," meaning I have a story to tell.

As is the native custom, everyone chants back, "ooooo-taka," meaning, "tell it," and the fun begins.

Africans have their own way of telling stories, and it almost always includes animals from the forest and a moral—sort of like *Aesop's Fables*. In this region, each animal has its own certain characteristics. The frog is very smart. The owl is dumb. Elephants are considered quite wise.

"This story is about an antelope," Papa begins. Shamba and Omba begin to nod and grin. They know this one well. Everyone settles in to listen.

"Now this antelope had such a beautiful daughter that everyone in the jungle wanted to marry her. The poor guy was at his wit's end dealing with all the offers for her hand. Who to choose from all the likely candidates? Like all fathers he wanted a suitor who was worthy of his heart's delight, someone with plenty of brains and brawn who would take good care of his girl.

"So he came up with an idea for a competition. Whoever could build a house for his daughter in one day could become her husband. The elephant asked to go first, and knowing elephants to be wise and strong, the father thought that was a good idea. He probably had the best chance of all the animals to complete the task. The elephant worked as hard as he could the whole day long, but failed to finish the house. It had good strong walls, but no roof. 'How would his daughter keep dry in the African rains without a roof?' the father asked.

"Next, the hippopotamus gave it a try. He, too, worked furiously at first, but as the day wore on, and the sun continued to beat down, the hippo got hotter and hotter. He moved slower and slower, thinking how good a cool dip in the nearby river would feel. A short break couldn't hurt, he thought, as he snuck off down to the riverbank. Before he knew it, nightfall had come and his house wasn't finished either.

"It was an impossible task, grumbled the elephant and the hippopotamus. No one could be expected to build an entire house by himself in one day. The father would have to think of something easier.

"But the antelope begged to be allowed his turn. Now the antelope knew that one antelope looks much like another, so before he started, he lined up his friends and asked them to help. They staked themselves out in the bushes out of sight, and as one antelope grew tired from the work, another would take his place. So it went all day long. Each worked so hard and fast that at the end of the day the house was built, and the first antelope won the beautiful daughter."

Papa pauses to let everyone enjoy the happy ending, but his tale is not quite finished. "So do you all know the moral of this story?" he asks.

Both Omba and Shamba smile knowingly and say something quickly in Tshiluba. The rest of us wait, expectantly, for Papa to translate.

"The moral is that it takes two fingers to pop a head louse," he says with a flourish.

Head lice! Yuck! African stories often seem to have surprise endings to us who come from another culture. But as I thought about the story and the moral, I began to see the point. In America, we might say, "two heads are better than one," or "it takes two to tango," or "he's not heavy, he's my brother," meaning that to accomplish some things in life, you need a little help from someone else. Problems are solved a lot easier when friends come to your aid.

We might come from different cultures, speak different languages, see life in different images, but underneath it all, we have the same human needs and know the same human truths. As I drifted off to sleep that night, I was still amazed at the wisdom of Papa's story.

The Voodoo Priest

When you build a hospital in a developing country, you really want that hospital to be the last line of defense against disease. Technically, you want to do the majority of your health care in clinics, rally points, clearings in the forest, and small villages so that you're not inundated with people who really don't need to be in a hospital but who could receive basic medical care, immunizations, and health education in their rural settings.

This pattern, which has worked well all over the world, seemed ideally suited for the Leogane District of Haiti. About an hour south of Port-au-Prince, the Leogane n District is a combination of medium-sized cities and small, rural villages.

This story happened in the village of Mercery, Haiti, a village controlled by the "Hunang," a voodoo priest. When we approached this man about the possibility of improving health care in the village—of cleaning up the water and providing some education in the areas of sanitation, family spacing, and basic nutrition, he simply refused. No health teams were going to enter *his* village. He declared that he owned that village. He controlled it, and he would take care of the people.

It didn't matter that none of the children were immunized. It didn't matter that they were all malnourished. It didn't matter at all that the water they drank came straight from a filthy stream that ran along a dirt road. None of those things mattered. The only issue that interested him was control. He had it—and he intended to keep it.

Another voodoo priest moved into the area and slowly worked his way over to Mercery. He had decided that there was room for two voodoo priests in the area. He figured he could practice as well as the other fellow, but it didn't work that way. Voodoo Priest "A" cut off the head of Voodoo Priest "B." So Voodoo Priest "A" was convicted of murder and sent to prison.

While he was in prison something wonderful happened. An elderly woman from the village of Mercery worked her way to our hospital. She came knowing that she was most definitely defying the wishes of her voodoo priest, but she was desperately ill, and he was in prison. This was the time to act. The hospital staff admitted her, and in their care, she began to respond to treatment. She was getting well, and she was also seeing a different way of living. While in the hospital, she decided that voodoo really wasn't the way to go for her or her village. She renounced voodoo and decided to start her life over.

Things were going famously until Voodoo Priest "A" paid his way off, got out of prison, heard about the woman's rebellion, and appeared at the front gates of the hospital. He declared that he was a voodoo priest of all power; the woman was taken from his village and forced into the hospital. He declared that—with all the power of a voodoo priest—he had come to reclaim the woman and take her back to the village where she belonged. It was his job alone to heal her.

Sometimes in developing (and even so-called civilized) countries, fear and superstition still hold sway. Tragically, some members of the hospital staff were persuaded by the voodoo priest's arguments. They released this courageous woman and sent her back to the village in the hands of the voodoo priest. He insisted that he would treat the woman and cure her. Instead, she died.

Her death made a powerful impact on all the villagers. They knew that the woman had gone to the hospital in opposition to the voodoo priest. They knew that while she was in the hospital, she was responding to treatment; she was getting well. They knew that the voodoo priest had paid his way off, gotten out of prison, and claimed that he would cure this woman. They knew he had taken her back to the village, and she had died at the hands of the voodoo priest.

Most importantly, the villagers knew that this woman was the mother of the voodoo priest. When he failed to save the life of his own mother, the villagers gathered around the voodoo priest to declare that as far as they were concerned, his power had been broken. He was out of business!

Today, if you go to the village of Mercery, you'll find a school for their children. You'll find a trade school for their adults. You'll find a program that provides a hot meal daily for the children so that they have a chance to grow up healthy. You'll find a well that has five spigots of clean water, and you'll find a clinic that's teaching the basics of health education, nutrition, family planning, and AIDS prevention. Oh yes, and you'll also find a voodoo priest, who still lives in a blue hut with a spirit pole outside his door—and spends his days pouting. He's remembering better times when he and voodoo were still in control.

Dhanyabad

There's nothing quite like Bangladesh in monsoon season. If the rain isn't falling down, the steam is rising up from the asphalt in steady waves. You get wet, you stay wet, and you might as well decide that it's okay to be wet in Bangladesh in monsoon season. Everybody else is. If the climate is so bad, why go there, you might ask? It's the people that make the difference in this country. They're so exciting, so alive, and so filled with surprises.

I had finished a meeting in Dhaka, the capital city of Bangladesh, and was taking a walk. The streets were filled with mud and puddles of water from the last rain. At the end of the street, some young boys were playing soccer in the mud. It was an amazing sight. How could they stay upright and keep from sliding? How did they know how to kick the ball to avoid the puddles? I had to get closer and watch.

I worked my way down the street, you know, trying to be inconspicuous, but they saw me and stopped the game. I walked up to this crowd of little boys and met with a delightful situation. One of the children was wearing a watermelon on his head. As if that wasn't unusual enough, he was also holding a badminton racquet and standing in the middle of a large puddle. I looked at the young boy and said, "Oh, I wish you could speak English. There are just so many things I'd love to ask you." You know, this part of the world was at one time a British colony.

The young boy looked at me, removed the watermelon from his head, took a deep breath, and said, "Well, I say, we all speak English here. Don't you?" I laughed so hard I forgot to ask him any questions. I just kept walking down the street chuckling. Bangladesh never fails to surprise me.

The day was a busy one. Our group was traveling from Dhaka to a place called Aladipuhr. That's in the Rajbari District across the confluence of the Ganges and the Brahmaputra rivers. To cross the ferry, we had to sit for hours waiting for the ferryboat. The heat was unbelievable. As we waited, crowds of people began to swell around us. They, too, were waiting for the ferry so that they could cross the river and get on with their business.

I guess I was daydreaming, more asleep than awake, as I leaned against the window of the truck. Someone tapped on the glass, and I jumped, taken aback. Standing at the window was a beggar. She was an elderly woman, and she carried on her hip her best friend, a woman severely deformed. I had seen them before and knew that they made their living going from vehicle to vehicle saying, "*Bakke, bakke,*" which means "give."

The coin she expected, and the one I gave, was called a *poisha*. Its value is about one-tenth of a penny. These women took my coin and gave the traditional answer, "*Dhanyabad,*" (which sounds like don-a-bot) and means "thank you." Then they did what I had seen them do before. They walked to a little shack about 50 feet from my truck, and they bought their food for the day.

What they bought was a rice cake. It was four-inches long and about two-inches thick. Normally, they would break the cake and share it. Then the older woman would carry her friend down to the river so that they could lap up some water. Most days, that would be their only meal. As expected, the two women had taken all the money (one-tenth of a penny) I had given them, and they had bought all the food they could buy with it (a single rice cake), but this time—they came back to my truck. They tapped on the glass again. I rolled down the window, thinking that they just wanted some more money. But they didn't.

Instead, these two precious women took all the food that they had, the rice cake, reached inside the truck, placed the food in my hands, patted me on the chest, and said again, "*Dhanyabad,*" then turned and walked away.

This was their way of thanking me for coming to their country to help them, for being a friend of the missionaries who worked there, for being their friend. And so, today, I want to say to you on behalf of the people of the world, *Dhanyabad, Twasakadilla, Merci beaucoup, Muchas gracias, Domo arigato.* …On behalf of the people of the world, thank you. Thank you for supporting the mission efforts of your church or giving to world charities. Above all things, keep it up. The job's not done yet.

No Snakes!

I don't like snakes. Let me be right up front about that. Everybody who knows me knows—I don't like snakes. Once I was standing in the courtyard of the Good Shepherd Hospital minding my own business, when I looked across the yard and saw a young boy. He appeared to about 12 years old, and he was walking diagonally away from me holding a stick in front of him at about a 45-degree angle. Something was obviously draped over the stick. I wasn't paying close attention until the young boy looked my way. He turned and started walking directly towards me. I could see then that the child had a snake draped over that stick! It was wiggling. I couldn't tell if it was alive or not, but it was wiggling. Have I mentioned that I don't like snakes?

As he got closer, I saw that the snake was about four feet long and very fat. He had a huge head and I could tell it was a Gabon Viper, a very poisonous variety. I didn't like the looks of him or want anything to do with him. As the young man continued to walk towards me, I froze. I just stood there staring at this child. As he got closer, he got a grin on his face. You know, the kind of grin that only a 12-year-old boy can get. The kind of grin that only a 12-year-old boy can get when he's up to something. This child walked up to me, and with a smile on his face, flipped that snake through the air right at me!

In your mind—I want to paint a picture. I want you to imagine not what I said, but what I did when the snake came flying through the air towards me. Let's just say that I didn't know that I could jump that high—and backwards, too. We're talking about an Olympic-record breaking, death defying, cow-jumping-over-the-moon kind of jump. Can you picture it? It scared me to death! I tell you that story, so you'll know I'm serious when I say, the worst possible thing that could go wrong on any expedition would have to involve a snake.

On one of our African adventures, Marcel came so well-prepared that he actually brought a handwritten book about all the plants and animals that we might encounter in that particular part of the world. Marcel is a Marine Corpsman. When he travels as part of the ROW team, he serves as our medic. His job was to look after my team as we explored the Sankuru River basin, and he took it seriously. Marcel had the ability to amputate a leg if he needed to out in the jungle. Fortunately, there hadn't been any major emergencies on this trip.

We had hiked out of the jungle up to the missionary hospital (and hostel), and most of us were resting. Marcel was purifying water out behind the kitchen. One of the missionary doctors came walking up to say that his gardener had killed a snake in his yard. He was carrying the limp reptile over a stick. He thought Marcel might want to identify it, since we hadn't seen that much wildlife in the jungle. Marcel couldn't resist the chance to use his book and tell the rest of us all about this African snake.

He watched as the gardener dropped the snake onto the cement floor. It remained motionless. As he bent to pick him up by the head, the *dead* snake spun around and bit him on the ring finger of his left hand. That's when Marcel remembered that a Puff Adder's only defense is to play dead. He immediately killed the snake and examined his finger. As there was only one mark, he figured that one fang had gotten him, and that it hadn't actually sunk into his finger but just grazed the surface. He removed his wedding ring, began forcing blood from the wound, and sent for help.

I couldn't believe it when someone came running with the news that a snake had bitten Marcel. A snake! Now? Here we were at the end of the expedition. We'd made it safely down the river and were expecting to fly home in a few days. I didn't believe it until I got there and saw my friend sitting on the ground in pain with his finger swelled beyond recognition.

In his cool, collected, Marine-medic voice, Marcel said, "The Puff Adder's venom has the power to kill four or five men with one bite. I would have cut off my finger immediately, but I didn't think the bite had really gone in deep. Obviously, I was wrong." The swelling was already creeping up his arm.

We made a frantic search of the hospital, but the only antivenin on hand was generic, not specific to Puff Adders, and it had expired several years ago. Marcel didn't think it would be any help. The only pain medication available was aspirin, but Marcel wouldn't take that because he knew it would thin his blood. He expected the venom to attack his circulatory system, causing him to bleed internally. Even though the textbooks said not to use ice, Marcel said to use it to try to slow down the swelling.

Marcel's arm swelled to the size of my thigh and turned as green as The Hulk. The pain was so intense that it would not allow him to sleep. We all prayed for him and tried to keep his spirits up with our usual joking around. Like a true Marine, he never complained about the pain or said he was afraid. He knew his chances of dying were great, and that there wasn't much any of us could do about it. Marcel began writing down the advance of his symptoms with the thought that the information might be useful to others.

Eventually, the pain was too great for him to write any longer. His body had turned black and blue from the toxin. The swelling was so great that we thought the skin would burst. You really wonder at a time like this—what do you say? Finally, I said the only thing that I could think of.

"Marcel, you are an active duty Marine. Is that right?"

"Yes sir."

"And you're assigned to me. Is that right?"

"Yes sir."

"And you've gotta do whatever I tell you to do. Is that right?"

"Yes sir."

"Good. Now, Marcel, I have *not* given you orders to die, so don't you die on me!"

"Okay."

And do you know what? He didn't die. After three days the pain finally peaked, and Marcel was able to get some sleep. When he awoke, the pain had subsided further. He knew that he had turned the corner. He was going to survive.

Now, I'd like to think that he lived because I was so clever in reminding him that he was a Marine and obliged to follow orders, but Marcel claims he was listening to a higher authority. "There's no way I should have lived after the bite of a Puff Adder. In my mind, the only reason I survived is because the *Man upstairs* wanted me to," he says. Since that time, Marcel knows that by his miraculous recovery he was given orders to live his life to the fullest and to continue doing God's work in the world. That's exactly what he has done.

When you think about it, aren't those the orders we are all given?

Learning to See

What do you see when you look in the mirror? Do you notice your blonde hair and brown eyes or a scar left by some long-forgotten accident? Or do you look beyond your features to catch a glimpse of the soul inside? As familiar as your face is to yourself and your family, it is hardly all there is to you. Haven't we all known some gray-haired, wrinkled, little old ladies who are young at heart? Despite all the blonde jokes, there are plenty of doctors who are beautiful and blonde. Some guys look athletic but are really in terrible shape. Appearances can be misleading, if not downright deceiving at times.

One thing I've learned from traveling the world and seeing so many different types of faces is to try to look beyond the outward appearance of a person and see what's on the inside.

ROW was first able to travel down the Sankuru River in the Congo because my good friend, David Law, lent us his ship, the *Kuto Misa.* David was always aboard, and it gave us an extra measure of confidence to have him along. As the son of missionary Burleigh Law, David had grown up in the Congo and loved to tell stories of his famous Dad.

Burleigh Law, known as *Uwandji Utshudi A Koi* (Chief Leopard of the Artisans) to his Batetela friends, served in the Congo from 1950 to 1964 and was killed trying to rescue missionary friends during a rebel uprising. He had spent eight years building the Lambuth Memorial Hospital. It was no easy task. All the heavy construction machinery (crates weighing tons) had to be unloaded by hand in Lusambo, then driven by truck 165 miles over the worst road in the Congo to Wembo Nyama. Even then, the machinery had to be assembled and everything adapted to work in the jungle. There wasn't a hardware store on the corner when you needed something. Fortunately, Burleigh had great mechanical talent, and he learned to improvise. Not even his father could fix everything, though, as David told us.

When David was a young boy, he and his family were traveling in their truck through the jungle and came upon another truck surrounded by a crowd of mostly women. Stopping to exchange greetings, the Law's learned that the truck belonged to Chief Kokolomami who was traveling to Lodja. They knew the chief was important because he owned a truck, but he was also famous for having 40 wives. At the moment, all of them seemed to be trying to push the truck and get it started.

Thinking that he could fix whatever was wrong, Burleigh lifted up the hood of the chief's truck to have a look. He stared inside for a short while, then closed the hood, shook hands formally with the chief, got back in his truck, and drove on.

"Dad, couldn't you fix the motor in that truck?" David Law wanted to know.

"Nope. It didn't have one!" Burleigh said with a chuckle. It seemed that whenever Chief Kokolomami wanted to go somewhere, he climbed up in the truck and made his wives push him through the jungle. He had a 40-women-powered engine.

Don't we all know people who are kind of like that? They look good on the outside, but if you lifted up the hood and looked inside there wouldn't be much there. You can't get the whole picture by just looking on the surface.

If you are ever in Port-au-Prince, Haiti, I hope you'll take the time to visit the Episcopal Cathedral there. It's a magnificent structure and such a contrast to the poverty and suffering that surrounds it. Inside, there's a grand mural of *The Last Supper*. The subject is familiar, but the perspective is a bit different. All of the disciples are gathered around the table with Jesus in the center in the usual fashion. But unlike most European artists' renditions, all of the figures are black, all save *one* of the disciples. Judas is white. We know that skin color had nothing to do with Judas's betrayal of Christ, yet how often do we view people with suspicion when their skin color or dress or language is different from ours? It gives you something to think about, doesn't it?

Near Pusan, Korea, there's a wonderful small town called Sunch'on, where you will find The Peace House. The Peace House was constructed as a home for people who are living out the last days of their lives with the long-term effects of Hansen's disease, better known as leprosy. They receive about $10 a month from their government, but the balance of their care comes from the Wilson Rehabilitation Hospital, established by Christian churches in South Korea.

Leprosy is very curable. There's no need to be afraid of it anymore but fifty to sixty years ago, it was a much more difficult disease to treat, in part, because the people who acquired the disease were ashamed to seek help and were hard to find. Only after a great deal of damage had been done by the disease did people make their way into churches and receive care.

Today, there are about 20 to 30 elderly people living in The Peace House, but they are a powerful witness to us all. What they have been able to do given their limitations is amazing. These people are blind and horribly disfigured. They don't have fingers, so they can't read Braille. Wanting to know and share the word of God, they had one option left. A group of them spent 25 years memorizing the entire Bible.

They are very humble people and afraid that you may be bothered by their physical appearance. Since they are blind, they don't look at you. They hold their heads down and wait to see how people respond. They've gotten to know me over the years, and I always respond by hugging and touching and laughing with them, letting them know that I am so grateful that they accept me, because I certainly accept them.

During one of our visits, they mentioned that they had memorized the whole Bible. I told them I couldn't believe it. I had the surprise of a lifetime. I learned firsthand that it takes 41 minutes to chant the book of James in Korean. We all sat on the floor, and they began rocking back and forth, chanting for all they were worth. I smiled and waved and jumped and danced about—their enthusiasm was infectious—and I figured they couldn't see how ridiculous I looked.

When they finished, one of them said, "Well, we've done one other thing we want to share with you. We've started a harmonica choir."

Fifteen of these very elderly men brought out their harmonicas and proceeded to play the most beautiful hymns and popular music. Watching them dance and perform, they are so filled with joy that you can't help but be swept up in their excitement and faith.

Being able to recite the Bible and play joyous music despite their disease, and the social ostracism that too often goes with it, would be remarkable accomplishments in themselves. But the story doesn't end there. They decided to take their talent on the road. The harmonica choir now travels the countryside of South Korea, performing music and reciting scripture for a good cause. No, it's not for people with Hansen's disease, as you might guess. The money they raise goes to an orphanage in Seoul, Korea, to help children who have been abandoned on the streets of that city—children that they say need some help, too.

Looking on the surface, these men had three strikes against them—they were old, they were blind and they were sick. By the world's standards, they were *out*. But the people who founded The Peace House didn't see them that way. Looking through the eyes of compassion and love, they saw people with brains, talent, and a contribution to make to the world.

My father once pointed out a very poor street person to me and said, "That man considers his life to be just as valuable as you do yours."

Enough said.

Peggy's Heartbreak

Peggy said she really did do pretty well, all things considered. It was just another day for her. She took the old Bronco and backed it out of her driveway. She opened the tailgate just like she'd done so many other times. She took a footlocker—a footlocker that was a little too heavy for her—but by grabbing both handles and swaying back and forth, she managed to get it into the back of the truck. It was time to go.

On this occasion, she was heading for a village called Coors. It's nothing more than a clearing in the elephant grass with a few thatched-roof, mud huts. She came to the village and backed the Bronco around to the little teaching area she had created by turning some logs into benches. Fifteen mothers were sitting there waiting for Peggy. As she got out of the truck, they greeted her in the traditional way.

"*Muoyo, Baba.*" (How are you, Madam?)

And she'd answer back, "*Malukai?*"(How are you doing?)

They'd all answer, "*Malumeempa.*" (We're doing fine.)

And then the whole crowd in a chorus would go "Ayyyyy-O!"

Peggy did as she always did. She greeted each mother individually, stroked the head of each child and then returned to the Bronco to open the footlocker. She started on the left as she always did. On the left-hand side she kept some little song sheets, which she handed out. The group always started by singing a few songs about having healthy children. She then produced what are called Path of Life cards. Peggy's health organization used these cards to plot the age and weight of the children, and to record immunizations, health concerns, and diseases.

She gave out two of the cards to new mothers who were just joining the group, and then she examined each child individually, talking all the while, "Oh, this baby has such bright eyes." "Ooooh, look at all the hair on this child." "This baby is growing so strong," she said of one infant who was struggling to get down. "Would you look at the tummy on this child? You're feeding that baby almost too much," she told another mother. "This child has a little rash. Well, I happen to have some ointment." "Has this baby been immunized before?" "We may need to see this child at the clinic. Could you come one day and bring your baby?" One mother and one child at a time, each pair received the attention of this gentle woman, who always wanted to be as encouraging and helpful as she could be.

She gave a short class on nutrition, talking about the importance of boiling your water before your child drinks it. She told them what to do if their babies got diarrhea—how to take one of the little packets of sugar and salt and mix it with a beer bottle full of boiled water. If they would give it to the baby, the baby would be okay.

She reached into the footlocker again and pulled out a hand trowel. She wanted to show mothers that this could be used to plant corn. She dug a small hole in the ground and placed a corn seed into it. Then she dug a hole right beside it and placed another corn seed in that hole. She then stepped over about 18 inches, dug another hole and planted corn in that as well. She then faced the mothers and said, "Okay, you tell me. Which corn will grow strongest, the corn that's spread out 18 inches or the corn that's planted side by side?"

All the mothers laughed. How could this woman from America who knew so much, know so little about corn?

"*Baba* Peggy, of course the corn that's spread out will grow the tallest and strongest. Everybody knows that."

And then *Baba* Peggy brought it home. "Well, just as corn grows best when it's spread out, so do our children. If you have one child and then another child and another child after that—then they won't get the nutrition, the strength, or the encouragement to grow straight and strong like corn that's spread 18 inches apart. If you wait a year or two years between each baby's birth, then those children will have a chance to grow straight and strong. Spacing your children means having healthy, strong children." The mothers understood just as they had understood about the corn.

"Oh, by the way, these hand trowels are very useful in your garden. Would anybody like to buy one?"

There was silence then, finally, an inquisitive mother asked, "Well how much do they cost?"

"How much do you have with you?" answered Peggy.

"Well, I have only a few cents."

"Ahhhh, oddly enough, that's how much they cost. And, today— today only, I'll give you a free bag of corn seeds with each hand trowel."

Now she could have given them away, but then they would have lost their significance. For each mother who had a few cents, this was a chance to own something. This was a chance to gain a little pride in having purchased a tool that would help her and her family survive in the very difficult African forest.

Once all the trowels had been distributed and the corn seed passed out, the songs sung, the babies praised, the immunizations delivered, Peggy closed the footlocker and pushed it back into the truck. She said she did fine as she closed up the tailgate and turned to face her friends. She said she was doing okay, when she opened her mouth to tell them what had to be told.

"*Baba,* today I had to pay $15 for a gallon of gasoline. We have clinics just like this throughout the province, but we don't have enough money to buy the gasoline to keep all of the clinics going. So we've had to make some tough decisions, and…well…we've decided that we can't keep this clinic open. I'm afraid this is the last time I'll be here, and I'm sorry."

She turned and she faced 15 horrified African mothers. She said she did okay as she turned and walked toward the Bronco. She did okay as she opened the truck door and got in. She managed to turn the key and start the truck. She was doing okay as she rolled down the window to let in a little air.

As she pulled off down that dirt road, she thought the worst was over and that she'd done okay, until she looked in her rearview mirror. Running behind her in the African dust was a young mother clutching her baby in her arm like a football and crying at the top of her lungs, *"If you leave, my baby will die!"*

It was not okay. In her heart, *Baba* Peggy had known it all along.

There are many organizations that bring aid and medical care and education to developing, war-torn, famine-ridden countries. They're advertised in magazines and on the Internet. You can find out about them from television or the radio. These organizations are making a difference in the world, one village, one mother, one baby at a time. I'd like to leave you with this challenge and this request. Please…please help them to turn their trucks around!

Boom-Boom to the Rescue

Let me thank you right now for reading my book. I'm sorry that we're not together in person so that I can tell you these stories. Part of the joy of sharing the experiences of my life is watching the way people respond. It's always exciting and sometimes has unexpected results.

I spoke in Memphis, which happens to be my hometown, and afterwards a man came up to me and said enthusiastically, "I want to help."

"Great," I responded, "What do you do?"

"Just wait. I'll send it to you," came the answer.

I soon found out that this man worked for a company that makes bubble gum. He sent me 300 pounds of bubble gum. My whole house smelled like the candy counter at a convenience store.

Now the gum came in 25-pound boxes. I have a lot of friends who go overseas and pitch in for us, so I decided I would just send each volunteer a 25-pound box of bubble gum. I sent a box to a neurosurgeon in Orlando, Florida, named Frank. He called me on the telephone to ask in his gruff and growling voice, "Mathes, what is this stuff?"

"What does it look like?" I laughed.

"Looks like a box of bubble gum," he said.

"That's gooood. You're a smart man, buddy. You figured that out all on your own. If I get sick, I'm gonna come to you."

Ignoring my sarcasm, he asked the obvious question. "Well, what am I supposed to do with all this bubble gum?"

"Frank, you're getting ready to go to Africa. Why don't you take the bubble gum and give it to all the children?"

"Hmmph," came the immediate reply. "I'm not going to Africa to give out bubble gum to children," and with those words, he hung up.

I wasn't fooled. I knew Frank's bark was a lot worse than his bite. And, sure enough, everywhere he went on that trip, his pockets were bulging with bubble gum. The children called it *boom-boom*, and he handed out *boom-boom* to all the little children he met. While he was giving out bubble gum one morning, Frank noticed a little boy who walked differently than the other children. He examined the child and discovered a tumor growing on his spine. If Frank didn't operate, the little boy would be paralyzed.

When someone can't walk in a developing country, you don't just go out and order a wheelchair. They simply don't exist. When an entire country is handicapped by poverty, disease, and the lack of basic living necessities, those with special needs have to fend for themselves. Just last summer, I saw a woman who for two years had been walking with sandals on her hands and dragging her body behind her, because she had neither crutches nor a wheelchair to help her get through life. I've watched little children roll from one point to another. More often than not, children whose legs don't work are simply allowed to die.

Frank knew that if he operated and made a mistake that the little boy would end up paralyzed anyway, but he knew that he had to try. Any chance at all of giving his patient a shot at a better life was worth the risk. And the risk factor was high. As you can imagine, this Congo hospital wasn't equipped with the latest technology. Even the electricity was erratic. There wasn't going to be a back-up team of specialists waiting in the wings if Frank ran into a problem.

Nevertheless, Frank put the little boy on the operating table and spent four hours getting to the tumor. He's good at what he does, and he got there safely, but by that time his patient needed more blood. He knew there was no blood bank at the end of the hall. There was no Red Cross office to call when supplies ran short. So Frank went to the little boy's mother and asked, "Would you give a pint of your blood to keep your baby alive?" Frightened, she ran out the door. She believed that if she gave blood to her son and he died, that she would die as well.

Fortunately, Frank's wife, Flossie, was along on the trip. Flossie spoke up and said, "Frank, you can take as much of my blood as you need—just keep this kid alive."

"Bless you. I'll take one pint. That's all."

He stabilized the little boy and went back to work. Four hours later, he got the tumor out. The operation was a success. Frank had the enormous relief of knowing that the little boy would be able to walk and run like other children. But right now, his body needed more blood.

Frank walked out of the operating room and into the waiting area of the hospital. Standing in front of the crowd, hitting his left arm with his right fist, he repeated for all to hear, "A-positive blood, A-positive blood!" People looked away. Others bent over to tie shoes that they weren't even wearing. Some simply got up and left the waiting area. Frank had reached the end of his rope—when he remembered that stupid box of bubble gum. He ran back to the house where he'd been staying. He grabbed the bubble gum, put it on a patient cart, and wheeled it into the waiting area. This time he entreated the group by alternately pointing to his arm and the gum on the cart, "A-positive blood—*boom-boom!* A-positive blood—*boom-boom!*"

Finally, a man came forward slowly rolling up his sleeve. "A-positive blood—*boom-boom?*" he questioned.

"Oh, you bet!" Frank grinned.

The man took two big ole scoops of bubble gum. He shoved them in his britches, and he gave a pint of blood. Do you know that I've played soccer with that little boy? He is alive and well, and that man, well, that man probably has a mouth full of cavities. So if you're a dentist, or know one, please get in touch with me. I'd love you to go to Africa and help out in a needy situation.

As Frank's experience illustrates, there are enormous hurdles to overcome in bringing better health care to the African Congo and other remote areas of the world. But if we dwell on the hurdles, we'll miss this story's very simple point. The point is, that we have to try. Who would have thought that a seemingly small and outrageous gift like bubble gum could help save a little boy's life? If that could happen—and it *did*—just imagine what you could do.

The Wake-Up Call

Well, no one told me that the lights went out at 11:00 o'clock, but they did. I was in a mud hut with a thatched roof in the jungles of Guatemala, and exactly at 11:00 p.m., I heard the generator in the distance sputter to a stop. The lights went out, and more importantly, the ceiling fan slowly ground to a halt.

When it stopped, the heat settled over me like a thick wool blanket, but I'm a jungle explorer. I pride myself on being prepared for most anything, so I was ready. I got out of bed, took a wash towel, dipped it in a basin of water, wrung it out, and put it over my head as if I had a fever. I climbed back into bed and fell sound asleep.

I was snoring away in a deep sleep, when something woke me abruptly. Newsflash: something was wrong! It wasn't a vague feeling of unease. It was a strong and insistent message. I didn't move a muscle. I started listening in case someone was trying to climb in the window or open my hut door. Outside one of the windows, I could hear crickets making their racket. That was good. Outside the door, I could hear an owl doing his owl thing, and that was good. We have these lizards that make strange noises in Guatemala, and they were making that awful noise, and that was good, too. All of those things together told me that there wasn't anybody trying to climb in the window or open the door.

That meant that whatever was wrong was already in the hut with me! Slowly, I reached over and took my flashlight from the bed stand and twisted it on. I decided I would shine it across the rafters first. I just knew there was a 700-pound snake hanging in the rafters about to have me for dinner. With a trembling hand, I slowly guided the light across the ceiling. There was nothing. Whew!!

I shone the beam down the left side of the bed. Nothing. Very carefully, I went down the right side of the bed, and there was nothing there either. Whatever was wrong must be at the foot of the bed.

I put the flashlight under my chin and lifted myself as slowly as I could—just in time to see a large scorpion climbing over my feet and heading up the sheets! I always travel with a metal coffee cup. It was sitting on the floor next to my bed, so I grabbed it and poured the water on the floor. I could deal with that later, I figured. I reached on the other side of the bed and got my sandal off the floor.

My plan was to hit the scorpion with the sandal and roll him over into the cup. I sat up, put the flashlight into my mouth, and taking the cup in one hand and the sandal in the other, reared back and hit the scorpion. He didn't move. I pulled back again. I hit him a second time, and all he did was hunker down and raise his tail. That undid me!!!

With rising panic, I hit him a third time, pried him loose from the sheet, rolled him over and got him into the cup. I put my sandal on top of the cup, sat it back down on the floor, and climbed back into the sheets.

My heart was beating like I'd run a two-mile race, and my mind was racing just as fast. Except for the usual night sounds, the rest of the village was still—everyone else was asleep. No member of our team had awakened me. I could only conclude that someone else had sent me an urgent message—and I believe that someone was God. To think that He cared enough about me to send a wake-up call to a hut in the Guatemalan jungle, that impressed me mightily. But it also impressed me that I had listened.

Before drifting back to sleep, I couldn't help but wonder if a scorpion that could withstand three whacks might be strong enough to lift the sandal off the top of a cup. I decided not to worry about it. At that moment, it was easy to trust that the line was clear and the call would come. I knew I'd be listening.

Comrades

Camping in the Congo isn't like camping anywhere else. It's more thrilling—always at the back of your mind is the thought that you are in a remote and not very civilized part of the world. Down deep, you know you must rely on your own wits, and those of your friends, for your comfort and survival. Never knowing what you may encounter adds a certain zest to traveling in Africa.

On one particularly busy expedition, I had returned to camp early to have a few minutes of quiet to myself. I thought I'd take a bath in the river and collect my thoughts, while the rest of the team worked in the village about a mile up the escarpment. The only other people in camp were Papa Akula, who was making preparations for dinner, and a soldier named Waro. He was from the rebel army and traveling with us.

Now I don't tell this to just anybody, but when I take a bath in the Congo, I either wear a knife or place it near me on the shore. It's a special nine-inch blade that Master Blade Smith Jimmie Buckner forged especially to fit my hand, weight, height and shoe size. Just kidding about the shoe size, but you get the idea. It's custom made for me. It usually stays in my camera bag when we're out in the jungle, but I take it bathing because it gives me a (false) sense of security in case one creature or another decides I'd make a tasty snack.

I was in the river standing up to my neck in the cool flowing waters. Papa was cooking, and our soldier was resting idly among the tents. It was a pretty normal afternoon. Then in the distance, I heard the sound of a dugout canoe filled with men coming our way. As they came around the bend, I noticed that there were about a half-dozen young guys in various stages of inebriation.

They saw our camp, and from the expressions on their faces and their hand signals, I could see that their intention was to stop and rob us. Had Papa Akula been in camp alone, the pickings would have been easy, but this time I was there, too. As fearless leader, I began laying plans.

Our camp was situated on a sand bar that was actually cut off from the bank of the mainland. The primary body of water flowed around the northern side of the sand bar, while a smaller offshoot flowed around the southern side to create an island. I was bathing on the side where the water flows fastest and deepest, because hippos and crocodiles don't like swift moving water. The canoe was headed down the narrower tributary, so I lowered myself in the water and began making my way around the island. My intention was to come up behind these men who obviously had evil intentions and catch them by surprise. I had the greatest confidence that the sight of a large, white man rising buck-nekked out of the water, brandishing a knife, and screaming at the top of his lungs would be enough to scare off the intruders. After all, it had always worked for Tarzan.

But as soon as our would-be, drunken-thieves pulled up to the island, their demeanor changed dramatically. Their loud and boisterous shouting turned to dead silence. They stared for a moment, then without a word, shoved off and floated downstream. I grabbed my towel and climbed out of the river to discover what had happened. I came face to face with our rebel soldier, who had been hidden from my view by the tents. He had dropped the bolt of his AK-47 rifle and was pointing his machine gun shoulder height at the retreating canoe. He was not smiling.

I patted him on the back and said a heartfelt, "thank you," as I retreated to my tent for my clothes. Waro earned his keep that day!

My last impression of this young soldier occurred as we were traveling down the Sankuru River. Andrae Crouch had written the song for ROW that I mentioned in an earlier story, and we'd finished filming a music video and were heading out of the Congo. We were on our way to Lodja and home. I had a portable CD/cassette-player with me. We played our music tape as we rode the river. The wonderful words of hope in the Crouch song made us proud to be serving our friends in the Congo.

As the song ended, our guest, President Onusumba Yemba Adolphe, of the *Rassemblement Congolais pour la Democratie,* had a request. He reached into his shirt pocket and handed me a cassette. He wanted to hear its music, and I played it for him. Celine Dion came on the cassette player singing, "O Holy Night." Her beautiful voice carried to the bow of our canoe and beyond. It had an effect on us I will never forget.

Though we were from Rwanda, the Congo, and America, we all knew the tune. As we each listened from our own context of life, it was as if a blanket of loneliness swept over each person in that dugout. I think many of us were missing those we had left at home. Music can do that. It can transport you from your surface thoughts to a deeper level of emotion or memory that you'd forgotten was there. We had been so wrapped up in helping our friends, taking care of the boat, the camp, and each other, that we'd lost track of our normal lives. Now there was a longing for home. Some of the young soldiers who had come to protect us knew they might never see their homes and families again.

I cannot help but wonder if Waro is still alive and if he's seen his family since that day. I hope so.

ROW Meets the Bully

Most people hear my stories after-the-fact—after I've had a chance to think about the experience, pare it down to the essential details and polish it a bit. If I'm going to be the one standing in front of the audience, well, I want to be as interesting as possible.

There are times, though, when you don't have time to prepare. You're caught in the middle of a story, and you just have to tell it as it unfolds. That's what happened when we traveled down to Belize in the fall of 1998. ROW had planned to beam a live expedition via satellite and the Internet to classrooms worldwide. We were going to introduce students to life in Belize, talk with the people, visit the jungle, see the Mayan ruins—I had an itinerary and script all set.

Mother Nature had other ideas. Our film crews never made it. Our plans all went awry, but through the miracle of e-mail we were able to share with students and our ROW family a very different, unscripted adventure. My friends tell me it was a pretty riveting story, so I'm going to share it with you the way I did with them—through excerpts from my unpolished, rambling, anxious e-mails from the eye of the storm.

October 25, 1998, Trip Day 2

"We may not be alone. Arriving in Orange Walk, we learned that an unexpected guest might stay awhile. The rainy season in Belize has started early this year. Along with the rain, there is now a layer of mud that swallows anything that gets in its way. We're talking about tires sinking a foot—tires swallowed by the stuff—back breaking, all-day-in-the-heat, pull-me-out-of-here, only-to-sink-again kind of STUFF!

"We may not be able to get to our base camp. It may be flooded. If the lower end of the lagoon is flooded, snakes and crocs will look for higher ground and that means base camp.

"But the worst visitor who just may intrude upon us is pretty serious and named Mitch. Mitch is a bully. Mitch likes to just beat up on things. He'll go to a farm, tear down crops, kill chickens, rip out the electricity, and dirty the water wells. He'll tear down wooden buildings and leave families without shelter. Mitch is a hurricane that is really picking up speed to the southeast of us. There is time to leave Belize and head for Florida.... If we stay, we risk losing all our gear, our vehicles, and possibly getting injured. If we leave, we leave behind all of our friends, their farms, homes, stores and wells.

"We need to make a decision. While part of me says we should join the flood of folks leaving the area, the majority of me says we are going to stay. It's 9:20 a.m. and we're gonna see if we can get to Honey Camp Lagoon. Just heard that the storm is expected to hit the Yucatan Peninsula. Get a map. Look us up. We are in the direct path of the storm. Where else do you expect to find ROW?"

As we traveled around Belize, helping people prepare for the hurricane, we visited the Presbyterian Day School in Cristo Rey. The kids there sent this message to our readers:

Dear Friends in America,

We are going to have a hurricane. Its name is Mitch. This is our last day of school for a while because of the hurricane. The Ministry of Education notified us by telephone that we should go home and get ready to look after our families and houses.

We will buy batteries for our radios, candles, matches, canned foods, water and protect our schoolbooks!!! If we don't, Miss Dorothy, our teacher, will get mad at us and that can be worse than a hurricane!! Her winds can be gusting up to 160 miles an hour—more than Mitch.

Please keep us in your thoughts for the next few days, especially— because we are scared.

It was signed by 14 children and "the best teacher in the world," Miss Dorothy.

October 26, 1998, Day 3

"We had to evacuate Honey Camp. The storm is coming and it is already a category 4, that's 4 out of 5! Camp is in a place we call "Oitmon" (out in the middle of nowhere), and if the rains really set upon us—we'd be stuck here and no help to anyone.

"The roads were pretty slick, so we crept along. A little boy with a huge bicycle was wrestling the thing down the road. He had a box of chickens strapped on it, heading to market. We piled the boy, bicycle, and chickens into the van. Many of you know how hard it is to peddle a bike in the mud. He was grateful for the ride.

"Part of ROW's outlook is that we must be flexible in every setting. We made our resources and technology available to the government of Belize and relief agencies. We are keeping all batteries charged up and good to go in case we lose power. We're going to help our friends board up their hotel to protect it from the storm as much as possible."

Knowing that we were facing high winds and flooding from the sea and rivers, I became upset watching the Weather Channel on cable in our hotel room in Orange Walk.

"Two separate announcers were discussing the hurricane. To their utter joy, they revealed to their audience that Jamaica had been spared the hurricane. "Looks like it's heading for Belize and the Yucatan. Now, for the weather in New York..."

"I was stunned. They talked about the hurricane hitting here as if it didn't matter! Once Jamaica and the Cayman Islands were safe, the big fear was whether or not it would hit the Gulf Coast.

"Let me tell you something! There are 210,000 of us in Belize. We have homes, base camps, families, cats, dogs, cars, businesses, and lives—just like they do in Jamaica and along the Gulf Coast.

"I learned a lot today by watching the Weather Channel. I learned the details of the hurricane. I also learned that it is important for us to realize that one part of the world is no more important than another. Whether the hurricane hits Belize or Brooklyn, we are all in this mess together. I don't think the folks on TV meant to be insensitive, but I wonder how they would have reported the path of the hurricane if they were here right now?"

October 27, 1998, Day 4

"The weather has really changed. Our American Embassy has asked us all to call and tell them our plans. We are in Orange Walk at the hotel. We are helping board up buildings, move belongings and animals. The whole coast of Belize is at risk. The term catastrophe is being used on TV.

"All flights have been suspended for the next five days in and out of Belize. Our film crews from the U.S. won't make it. The water on the bridge is already half again as high as it was [this morning]. Our room is full of canned stew, Spam, potato chips, cereal, olives, canned juices, and fruit. Tomorrow we will buy bread—the bakery is working all night to feed as many as they can.

"Our goal right now is to prepare for the hurricane...and to offer assistance to those injured in the storm, left homeless, or otherwise in trouble. I'm glad you're with us. Quite honestly, our team doesn't feel so alone knowing you are on the other end of the line.

"Life is an adventure. We thought we were coming to Belize to entertain you and share our explorations with you. It turns out, that we have come to this place at a time when we may in fact, be needed by a great many people. That's what ROW is all about."

And later, "Spent the day moving hotel furniture to the second floor in case of flooding. Also moved a kinkajou, ocelot and weasel to higher ground—good luck guys. Some fellow on American news keeps saying how grateful he is that winds have died down from 180 to 165 miles per hour—easy for him to say! Rain just appears and it's getting harder and harder; winds are really beginning to blow.

"Found out we can get a phone line out—but the server is down in Belize City, so we can't e-mail over the phone lines. Bill and I found out we can take the satellite phone and reach a satellite even through the glass of our van window—will be a way to reach you—even in the storm.

"We are safe. Those in straw and thatch houses are not. Remember them in your thoughts."

October 28, 1998, Day 5

"We've just made the rounds around town. Refugees have moved into local churches, schools, and homes. A friend has four families living with him, as they wait for Mitch. We've noticed that kids have very little to do during this lull in activity.

"We met with several teachers this morning and discovered that books are a great need for Belize—so I have an idea. What if we get permission from the Belize government for the following: We ask schools across America to gather footlockers of books and raise $50 a footlocker for the shipping. We put the footlockers in a 40-foot [shipping] container and ship them to Belize. Then we build small libraries around the Orange Walk district.

"We could make a huge difference in the education of the kids in this part of the world. Are you interested? So, in spite of the hurricane, let's look ahead to helping students in Belize!"

We decided to go see how the nearby Mayan ruins were faring in the storm. They were faring better than we were as my cryptic message shows.

October 29, 1998, Day 6

"We had to leave the ruins—too much rain—so we are hiding in a cave five feet high and 10 feet across—FULL of bats! They keep flying past me, and it's awful!"

October 30, 1998, Day 7

"There are times when we ought to think things through! Yesterday we took off to check on the New River for flooding, people at risk, and the Mayan ruins at Lamanai. Antonio (our guide) took us in his 23-foot, open boat...for two hours we wound our way through the mangrove [swamps] and jungles...the first creature we spotted was a crocodile, waiting in the shallows. He didn't seem to mind our presence, until we got within six feet or so. He slashed his tail at us and slid off towards the depths. Iguanas draped themselves across tree limbs and just stared at us. The largest was a six-foot, brown iguana with four-inch spikes...he looked spooky, but they are really very docile. We passed a large gathering of lily pads, where bright-winged jacana birds danced and flapped their wings at us. Herons, egrets, snail kites, brown jays, and yellow-headed parrots filled the skies—in spite of the storm.

"The river was wild and swollen. With hardly a second's notice, the rains caught us. We stowed our gear, grabbed plastic bags, and climbed into them. I tore a hole for my head and arms and settled in for the trip. Tropical storms are COLD! The rain comes fast and stings your face and eyes. For the better part of our ride, the rain pummeled us. We were soaked to the skin before we even arrived at Lamanai!

"After a quick lunch of cold hot dogs and wet bread, we tried to e-mail. We made a tour of the ruins to make sure they had survived the storm and that caretakers were in good shape. As we hiked from ruin to ruin, we were followed by the roars and grunts of howler monkeys. Troupes of howler monkeys claim their territory by calling out threatening sounds that carry for three miles or more!

"This jungle at Lamanai has become a refuge camp for most of the mosquitoes in the world—the rain washes off our bug *goo*. Now I know why the howler monkeys are howling!

"We left early to continue our search for storm victims along the river. The flooding was so high that farmers had boarded their homes (or chained them down) and moved inland. Every farm was deserted. I was glad and hoped the families were safe.

"Things got really rough when the storm returned. I didn't know it could rain so hard, for so long! For over an hour and a half, we were beaten by the driving rains—then it got dark! When the sun went down, it got really cold. Antonio had no lights and maneuvered the boat by lights reflected from the clouds. We ducked, shoved, and pushed our way through narrow channels. We stopped beside a tree, and Antonio told us to look for the bats. Ugh! We searched every limb, but couldn't find them. Antonio just smiled. The bats were right beside us, less than a foot away. Eight or nine bats took off around us. Whew! Trick or treat!

"We managed to find Orange Walk in the dark. With backpacks strapped on, we hiked down Main Street. Everything is boarded shut. The streets are empty. Who in their right minds would want to be out hiking in a tropical storm?"

October 31, 1998, Day 8

"The hurricane passed us by, but the storm flooded a lot of homes and land. We have been riding around checking for damage and talking with village leaders about our library idea.

"Returning to Orange Walk, we crossed an overflow creek that had been transformed into a swimming hole. People of all ages were busy jumping, diving, and enjoying the water.

"Belizeans have a wonderful attitude about life. Hurricanes, floods, heat, wind, and bugs never slow them down! They are committed to educating their children and would love books in English. I hope we can help."

November 4, 1998, Day 12

"Belize is setting a great example for the rest of us! We've just left the town square, where hundreds of people are bringing thousands and thousands of pounds of food and clothing for the relief efforts in Central America. The worst of Hurricane Mitch missed Belize but devastated its neighbors. [Central American officials estimated that 7,000 died in floods and mudslides triggered by the storm.] 'Tu y Yo Radio,' 102.1 FM, in Orange Walk and 98.5 FM in San Pedro are hosting a spirited event that includes music, good moods, and sharing, sharing, sharing! I've never seen anything like it in my life.

"Belize is made up of people of all races and beliefs. They are a wonderful example of tolerance and magnificent generosity. Folks of all ages are bringing bags of clothes for direct shipment to Honduras, Mexico and Guatemala."

November 5, 1998, Day 13

"Tomorrow we leave Belize. Orange Walk is like home and I will miss Ena, our staff person, and all her family. We will miss our many friends.

"Going home is so special. Two weeks away is a long time. I can't wait to see my wife, Dr. Mik (a college professor at Brenau University), and our sons, Benjamin and Adam. Adam has the role of Reverend Hale in the play, *The Crucible*. He starts tonight, and I am here in Belize. I called him to wish him luck, but it's not the same as being there with him. Hopefully, I'll be in the audience on Saturday night. Mik has been dealing with the builders as we build a new home in north Georgia. Benjamin is at the University of Georgia. He cut his toe playing Frisbee and has 8 stitches. Our dogs, Winston and Alexander, miss me very much. Mik tells me that when Winston passes my Land Rover, he sits by his door and waits for me to open it.

"Everything in life is a swap. I swap missing my family to be in the bush trying to do good. It's not easy, but if we don't get involved, things will never change. I guess that's what ROW means to me. It's a chance to get involved and make a difference in the world."

*   *   *

Well, that's my story about Mitch, the bully. Like a lot of bullies, once we were prepared to face him, he turned tail and headed another way. We never got to do our telecast, but something wonderful did come of that trip. Our friends responded overwhelmingly to ROW's idea to build libraries. Since then, we have shipped thousands of books to Belize. The books went to nine villages where the people loved the idea of their children reading and learning more about the world!

The Village of Kongololo

Let me take you to the village of Kongololo. How can you resist a name like that? Let's see, under normal conditions—when there is no war on—you would start by catching a flight to Brussels, where you would most likely be able to connect with a flight to Kinshasa, the largest city and capital of the Democratic Republic of Congo. This port city on the Congo River was founded and named Leopoldville, in 1891, by Henry Morton Stanley, the explorer known for finding David Livingston and the source of the Nile, not to mention traveling the entire length of the Congo River, but that's another story.

As you can imagine, Kinshasa has grown and changed a lot since Stanley's day. You may want to have someone meet your plane and help you through customs, because the airport will be filled with people in every costume imaginable, and they'll be speaking French, Swahili, Kikongo, Tshiluba, Lingala, and any of the other 200 Congo languages and dialects.

If the airport is overwhelming, the city will put you into emotional overload. There are roughly seven million folks crowded into Kinshasa, which has for years been ravaged and devastated by violence, pillaging, and disease. Many of the colonial office buildings are in ruins and serving as makeshift housing. There is no sanitation, no safe water supply, no trash pickup, and only intermittent electricity. Since sending a child to school is financially out of reach for most families, children beg on the streets or sell what they can find and balance on their heads. Health care is primitive, costly, and scarce. Kinshasa is a city with so many critical needs.

Leaving the city, you'll fly 500 miles across country to Kananga in the heart of the Kasai Province, a land of diamond and copper mines, jungle, and lush savannahs. If you have called ahead, someone with a pickup truck will take you to spend a night at the guesthouse of Good Shepherd Hospital, about 12 miles out of town in the village of Tshikaji.

From there, you'll need to take a bush plane to Lusambo, a decaying port town on the Sankuru River. The river is important. Since there are few roads to outlying settlements in the Congo anymore, you'll need a boat, some camping gear, a water purifier, some food, bug spray—a guide is a good idea, too! Then all you have to do is paddle up the Sankuru River for several days, and there you are—the village of Kongololo (pronounced Congo-lu-lu). Now wasn't that easy?

Well, of course not! If it were easy, the civilized world would have put a pharmacy and a Super Wal-Mart on the corner, and there would be no need for humanitarian efforts, like Rivers of the World, and the people who support them. Getting into this remote area is a challenge, but now that you've come this far, you have arrived at one of my favorite places in the whole world.

It's hard to describe how beautiful the Congo can be. Every morning there's fog on the river that shrouds the jungle in an ethereal mist. Sometimes it can give you quite a shock to have visitors in canoes suddenly appear out of the fog to see what you're doing on their sandbar. They're curious, but friendly. As the mist clears, you'll see African gray parrots and the occasional hornbill flying overhead. You hear birds off in the forest and drums pounding as you pass the villages, maybe laughter from village children who play in the river shallows. Villagers who know us will often come out to the banks to sing and clap as we pull up, giving us a warm, African welcome.

One of my favorite parts of traveling in the Congo is establishing camp on sandbars along the Sankuru River. We unload the boat and set up our tents. We arrange them so that everyone is protected and as safe as can be from any wandering animal that might be in our area. Papa Akula always establishes his kitchen near the river's edge—closer to the dishwasher that way. He gets a fire going, and we know that there will be something tasty stewing by the time we get back to camp. While Papa cooks, the rest of us visit nearby villages, hold clinics, distribute medicines, and show movies. Though filled with hard work, most of our days are peacefully uneventful. Not always, however, as you'll soon read. Our last visit to Kongololo is one I'll never forget.

We left base camp that morning to travel down river about 45 minutes to the village. It sat on top of a hill, so we hiked up the trail carrying our supplies to a central meeting point. A very kind, blind chief and his sons came out to meet us. We paid our respects and offered him gifts of Bibles. The chief accepted them graciously and opened his village to our team.

For the next five hours, Doc Marcel Telders, Freight Train, Lou Anne McCrae, Kevin Corcoran, Laura Strange, Dr. Jean Ngoyi, Chris Price, his daughter, Lauren, and Dr. Paul Law were busy running our traveling clinic. Everyone in the village had parasites and many were infected with horrible worms. Handing out medicine that would take care of many of these problems was a simple matter, but invaluable. There are no doctors, medical centers, or drug stores in the area, and the people have no money for medicines. Getting needed pharmaceuticals one thousand miles into the jungles of the Congo is a major undertaking, but one that is deeply appreciated.

Towards the end of the afternoon, we cranked up a generator and hooked it to a video projector. We showed a movie called "The Jesus Film," all about the life of Christ. This one movie has been translated into hundreds of languages, and we show it either in French or Lingala. Many residents of the Congo are Christian, thanks to missionary efforts of many denominations that continue in the area to this day.

It probably doesn't come as a surprise that the people in the village of Kongololo never get to see movies. They were spellbound as they watched the life of Christ unfold before them on the screen. Watching the emotion on their faces and the tension in their bodies as they followed along, empathizing and almost acting out parts of the story, was a moving experience for them and for us.

I had stepped apart to photograph the event, when I noticed that coming fast behind us was a large, black cloud rolling down from the hills towards the village. I knew that the cloud carried a tremendous rainstorm, and I didn't want it to interrupt our movie presentation. As I stood there watching it advance, I started talking to it. John Wayne had nothing on me! In my most commanding voice, I said something like this, "Now look, we've come a long way to show this movie. If you come blowing in here right now and disrupt things, these folks aren't going to get to see the end of the Jesus film, and I'm going to be really bent out of shape. So you just stay right there!"

As I was talking to the storm, Mike Reinsel walked up and asked me what I was doing.

"Well, Mike, I'm trying to tell this storm to stay right there, because I don't want it to upset things. We've come so far, and these folks need to see this movie. Heh, why don't you help me? You stand here and talk to it, too."

Mike commented that while he knew plenty of people who could talk "up a storm," this was the first time that he'd met anyone who talked "to a storm," but he was agreeable and said, "okay." So now there were two of us watching and talking to the storm, telling it to just stay there until we were finished what we were doing. Amazingly, it listened! We were able to show the rest of the film, pack our bags, and start down the path towards the boat.

As we were walking back down the hill, the storm came rolling in with a vengeance. Suddenly, the wind was howling. The trees were just about bent over. The thunder was ear shattering and the lightning, literally, danced all the way across the sky. We were down in a river basin, so the expanse of sky was huge. You could see the jagged streaks as they traveled from one side of the horizon to the other. After each flash, the sky went black. We were piling into the boat as fast we could go, and then it dawned on all of us that we had to go about an hour back upstream in order to reach our camp. Being in the middle of the river with the storm raging all around was terrifying.

So of course the first thing we did after climbing into the boat was sing "Dixie." That's the song we sing when we're scared. Sitting in the back of the boat overlooking all the heads of our team, I also started praying.

"Now, Lord, I just bought all this camera equipment. It cost a whole lot of money. If you let this boat get hit by lightning, and it starts to sink, you're going to expect me to save Chris. But if I let go of this camera equipment, the trustees are going to be really mad at me. I can't hold it and grab Chris at the same time, so I just want you to know that if you hit the boat with lightning, Chris is probably going to drown—cause I'm going to save this camera equipment!"

It's terrible to admit that I was so concerned about equipment at a time like that, but it's true. Fortunately, I never had to make the decision. We didn't get hit by lightning, and we all made it back to base camp, drenched, but safe.

But the adventure wasn't over yet. As we landed, Papa Akula sprinted past us. He was racing to cover up all his pots and pans, the food, and all our supplies before the rains destroyed everything. The wind was blowing so hard that we watched one of the tents rolling end over end toward the edge of the sandbar. A few of us jumped out of the boat to chase it down before it landed in the river. The rest of the team was frantically trying to gather their belongings and get inside their tents, where they would be safer from the downpour.

As we were dragging back the runaway tent, Chris and his 19-year-old daughter, Lauren, came running up to tell me that their tent had blown away. "Ben, we can't find it anywhere," said Chris.

"Well, jump in the tent with me. We've gotta get out of this storm!" I yelled.

No sooner had we jumped into my tent than Lauren spoke up and said, "Oh, Uncle Ben. It smells sweaty—like a boy in here."

"Well, Lauren, what did you expect? I didn't know I was going to have company," I said with an attempt at humor.

"It's nasty in here and it's full of sand. I can't stay in here," she persisted.

Falling into my parental tone, I snapped, "Lauren nobody else offered you anywhere else to go. Quit complaining."

"No, I'm not staying in here! You have to get the sand out," was her teenage reply.

So in the middle of the storm, I pulled my stuff out, picked up the tent and shook it so that this dear, sweet child could be happy climbing into my very small shelter. While I was knocking the sand out of the tent, Chris managed to find their footlocker with all their gear in it. No sooner did I set the tent down and throw my footlocker into the opening, than Chris and Lauren began to unfold their sleeping pads. (I ain't got no sleeping pad, I thought testily.) They rolled out their sleeping bags complete with the little covers that went over them, and then Lauren topped it all off by asking, "Daddy, where did you put our satin pillows, you know, the ones that we found that were not too big, not too small, but just right?"

I swear this is a true story!!

Well, once Lauren and Chris had climbed into my two-man tent and into their sleeping bags, I was invited back in. I had about eight inches on one side to sleep. My luggage had been shoved over to my side so that I couldn't even stretch my legs out. Lauren and Chris had taken sleeping pills and were snoring like lumberjacks. I was hot, tired, sweaty, crammed into my tent, turned sideways, unable to stretch out, and I lay there thinking, Lord, what did I do to deserve this?

Do you ever do that—look for someone else to blame for your own problems? Anyway, as I lay there uncomfortable and very much awake, the Lord suddenly made it all crystal clear. "Look, when you were back in that village, if you'd had any sense, you'd have told that storm to completely go away," said the Sovereign voice in my head.

"Unfortunately, you didn't. You just told the storm to sit there until the movie was over. So that's where it sat until you were leaving the village—and *then* it hit with full force. And then you had to dance through the lightning all the way down the river. But I let you live so that you could get back to camp safely and be forced to share your tent with Lauren and Chris (whom as you know, snore like banshees), just so you could stay up all night long and think about the fact that your prayers were too small."

He had me. There was no use arguing the point. If I had prayed for the storm to completely disappear, Chris and Lauren wouldn't have lost their tent. We wouldn't have been scared out of our wits on the river. I

wouldn't have been concerned about the new camera equipment or anyone drowning. And right at that very minute, I would have been sleeping
peacefully under the Congo stars, instead of enduring the racket of the
noisy twosome.

My prayers had been too small, but by the end of that long night, my
faith had grown a notch or two.

A Cultural Dilemma

I'm not sure it was what Miss Manners would have done in this situation. To be honest, I didn't have a copy of her etiquette book with me and wouldn't have had time to look up the answer anyway. I've found that when you travel to different parts of the world, a lot of times you just have to wing it.

In Bangladesh, I had friends who were teaching agriculture to the residents there. One of the men who came to the agricultural school had a wife and 19 children. I can't remember if all of the children were his, but it didn't matter. All of them were his responsibility to feed and look after.

I can't begin to imagine the challenge of feeding a family that large, but my agricultural friends worked with him patiently and steadily. They taught him how to create a farm from the three acres of land that he owned. He had to work without the aid of commercial fertilizers (which he couldn't afford). By mastering new farming methods, this man learned how to grow enough food to feed his entire family eleven months out of the year without having to get a second job. Do you think he was proud? I've never seen anything like it! He couldn't wait to invite us to his farm for a celebration.

In Bangladesh, a celebration is called a function. We knew this was a very important event for this family, so we arrived on time. The family hung wreaths of flowers around our necks and served us cookies made with almond paste. Almond is one of those very distinct flavors that you either enjoy, or you don't. I'm of the latter persuasion, but my mama taught me manners, so I took one to be polite.

After the refreshments, all manner of speeches were given and acknowledged, as we stood in the broiling Bengali sun. Then the man stood at attention with his family and posed for pictures. I thought that would be the end of this elaborate function, but the farmer did something very generous. He offered me a very large coconut to drink.

Such a touching act of generosity inspired me to drink the entire coconut's contents, so he would know that I appreciated the honor. Now this was a huge Bengali coconut with more than a quart of coconut milk in it. I managed to drink the whole thing, and my friends told me to make a big show of how much I enjoyed it, so I did. I licked my lips, flashed a wide smile, wiped my chin on the sleeve of my shirt, and gave a large satisfied sigh—Ahhhhh! I was the very picture of a man who had never been so pleased with a coconut.

I must admit, I was feeling pretty pleased with myself. Without knowing the language or all the customs of the country, I had risen to the occasion. I had managed to show that I valued the gift and honored my host. Mission accomplished, I thought, and now to find some shade and a little rest—but not so fast.

My actions had been so convincing that the man just naturally assumed that I must want another coconut.

"No, no, no, my friend," I said kindly, all the while motioning that I couldn't possibly do justice to another one. "Thank you, but no…." I said.

He answered, "No, no, you my friend," and persisted in pushing the coconut towards me.

I pushed it back, saying again, "No, no thank you, my friend. You're my friend, but—."

Each time I'd begin to make excuses, he would repeat the litany, "No, you my friend, you my friend," all the while pushing the coconut towards me.

As we went back and forth with this exchange, my agricultural friends stood by trying to stifle their laughter and doing absolutely nothing to help the situation.

"Okay," I finally agreed. I took the coconut and tried to drink it by surreptitiously pouring most of it down the front of my shirt. Now bear in mind that it's awfully, awfully hot in Bangladesh. If you're already sweaty and smelly, pouring a little coconut milk down your shirt does nothing to improve matters. Now I was sweaty, smelly, and sticky. But I managed to polish off the libation, and my friends enjoined me, again, to make a show of my enjoyment and appreciation of his generosity. With a little less enthusiasm, I did as instructed.

His response was to get yet another coconut and shove it in my direction, exclaiming, "My friend, my friend—."

I looked at him and said, "No thank you!" and pushed it back at him.

He kept coming at me with the dreaded sphere and the same refrain, "My friend, my friend…"

This time I looked him right in the eye and said, "Look, I'm you're friend, but I'm not going to drink this coconut, and if you keep insisting, I'm going to bash you on the head with it? Got it?"

Maybe it was the frustration in my voice or the flash in my eye. Anyway, he looked at me, said, "Okay," raised the coconut, and drank it himself.

"Ah, you my friend," I laughed, and we parted as such.

Manners help in a lot of situations, but when it comes to real communication between peoples of different cultures, languages, and countries, a little honest emotion can go a long way towards establishing a bridge. I find I have a tendency, sometimes, to be too subtle in my communication skills. I'm learning to speak up. Everyone understands "no!" And everyone understands "yes!"

First You Need a Boat

The mist had cleared, and the sun was beating down hot and steady as only it can in Africa. Video camera in hand, I was filming the river, but I could hear the steady stamping of feet hitting the wet sand, the thud of boxes being loaded, and the easy bantering of guys up for adventure.

"Is this what it looked like in the brochure you got?" Thomas asked Marcel, pointing to the boat.

"Nah, mine had pictures of girls lounging by the pool. Must have been a different *Kuto Misa*, huh?" Marcel yelled loudly in my direction so I'd be sure and here.

"Yeah, I think they sent us the African Queen by mistake," came the reply.

"Nope, I've seen the African Queen," chimed in Paul. "It's in better shape!"

I just laughed. Nothing could dampen my spirits at this moment. I was finally on the banks of the Sankuru River in the Congo loading the boat that would take us into uncharted territory. You see if you're going to be a jungle explorer in this part of the world, first you need a boat—and mine had come chugging into port early that morning. It had only taken six years.

This story actually began with my visit to Chief Ikongusamu of the Dekesee tribe in the village of Bolumbo. You remember the story of my eating fast food in Africa? We call it fast food because you sort of have to bat it around a bit to keep it on the plate. I told you about how sick I got from eating too many smushed termites. What I didn't tell you was that my visit with the chief so touched my heart that I promised I would come back. The Sankuru River was beautiful and seemed to flow on forever. Standing on its bank, I couldn't help wondering what life was like along its banks. Those wonderings and my promise stayed with me.

Maybe I had read too many accounts of Stanley, Livingston, and early missionaries to Africa, but I had managed to talk my good friend, Thomas, into exploring the Sankuru River with me. We thought maybe we could buy a large canoe, transport it to Africa, and find our way around by using a watch chronometer. It was exciting talk, but we both had jobs and families, so our plans never came to pass.

Then one day I was sitting in a meeting with a Congo missionary named David Law. He had a boat that he'd used to transport coffee to market when the economy had been better, he told me. Can you imagine how my ears pricked up at that? He knew the Sankuru River and would love to take us down it. Did I jump at the chance? You bet!

I recruited a team of friends in the United States. We trained in the Okefenokee Swamp of southern Georgia, battling mosquitoes and learning how to use a global positioning satellite (GPS) system. (AAA doesn't make road service calls to the Congo. In case of an emergency, we needed to be able to tell a bush plane pilot how to locate us.) We had so much fun that about half the recruits quit on the spot, but the other half said, "Yes, let's go!" So here we all were in Lusambo, attempting to load about 100 footlockers of supplies into a 30-foot, deep-well, coffee barge with a thatched-roof canopy.

We had been thrilled to see the *Kuto Misa* steam full speed through the mists into port that morning. What a glorious sight! She hadn't been there the day before, and we thought our trip might have to be aborted, so it was a great relief that our ride had shown up. Now that we'd seen her close up—in the full light of day—she seemed a bit weathered, to put it nicely. Ship captain Shamba explained their delay. The boat had been moored for a long time in Bena Dibele about 100 miles upstream. When he and Akula had gone to get her, they found that neglect and the rainy season had created a disaster. The boat had sprung leaks and sank to the bottom of the river.

After recruiting villagers to help raise her and get her running, the two men had arrived in Lusambo only a day late. Now there was another hitch. Since it was dry season in the Kasai Province, about 300 yards of mud separated the dock from the river. The mud was too soft to support a truck, so we were loading the boat on foot.

"What is all this stuff," Paul Law kept asking.

David's son, Paul, had grown up in the Congo. He was a medical student in the states, interning to be a pediatrician. He planned to come back to work in the Congo once his training was complete and jumped at the chance to conduct a health survey with us along the Sankuru River.

Many of the boxes were healthcare supplies, but the rest was "stuff" for the camp.

"I like a comfortable camp," said Thomas, who in hiking boots, wick-proof socks, khaki shorts, and hunting vest looked like he'd stepped out of an L.L. Bean catalogue. He had packed a comfy, inflatable mattress pad and all manner of camping gear. We carried a water-purification system, the GPS system, VHF-radios so that we could talk to each other between camp and villages, screen rooms for sleeping, tools, flashlights, fishing gear, bug goo, and assorted treats from home—peanut butter, GORP and POWER Bars.

Paul just shook his head. He had come to the wilds of Africa equipped only with his medical bag, shorts, t-shirts and flip-flops.

When everything was finally on board, the crew began to claim spots on the boat amidst all the baggage.

"I could have sworn I'd paid for a luxury cabin," grumbled Chris, finding a bare spot at last between the tents and food storage bins.

"Well, then, no doubt you'll be dining with the captain on the quarterdeck tonight. I hear cocktails are at 6:00. Black tie, of course," shouted Marcel, over the steady chugging of the engine.

"And just where might they be hiding the quarterdeck on this barge?" Chris asked.

As you can see, I was traveling with a real bunch of comedians. They'd already learned that humor goes a long way to easing the fears and discomforts of exploration.

But all jokes aside, we were underway at last and settled in for a close-up view of jungle...then some more jungle...followed by still more jungle. This is not a populated area. Occasionally, someone would spot a gray parrot or someone in a dugout, and we'd all get excited and break out the cameras, but for the most part, we just chugged along for six hours or so.

As night fell, we were all watching for a sandbar to make camp on, when we bumped into one—literally. The *Kuto Misa* was stuck! Led by our native crew, the guys climbed overboard one by one to try and push her free. This is just great, I thought, our first adventure. I immediately pulled out the tape recorder and began interviewing for the folks at home.

"Yes, folks, here we are stuck on a sandbar on our first night out on the Sankuru River. Not to worry—because our intrepid team has things under control. Tell, me Chris, what's it like down there in the water?"

"Mathes, I'm going to kill you!" he yelled back.

But then the boat suddenly lunged off the sandbar and everyone scrambled aboard—that is everyone except Marcel and Chris. One minute they were chest deep in the water, and the next minute, they just seemed to disappear. We were drifting away in the fast current and after a moment of shock, they began to swim after us.

The night was dark and the water darker. I didn't know what kind of nasty creatures were underneath and didn't really want to think about it. We were in the middle of nowhere, and I was scared that we might lose them, but as leader, I couldn't afford to panic. So I called as calmly as I could.

"Okay, I know you guys are having fun, but we can't hang around here all night. Quit dawdling, now, I know you can swim faster than that," and anything else I could think of. I'm sure Chris would have yelled back something rude, but he was swimming with his watch in his mouth. After what seemed like hours, but was probably minutes, they got close enough for us to pull them back into the boat.

Relief! I could see it written all over Chris's face and knew my own must have looked the same. I expected some sarcastic comment about my recording instead of helping, but as soon as Chris caught his breath, he said, "Did I call this boat a barge? My mistake. From the drink, it looked like a luxury liner," he said.

"You got that right. Even without a quarterdeck, she looks pretty good to me," echoed Marcel. "Yep, I've got newfound respect for the good ole *Kuto Misa.*"

Perspective. Have you ever noticed how big a part that plays in how we act and feel? Hot coffee seems like a small luxury, unless you're caught outdoors in a snowstorm. A three-bedroom house seems like middle-class to most of us, but compared to a thatched hut, it's a mansion. After a swim in the cold, murky waters of the Sankuru River, the *Kuto Misa* seemed like a haven. No, she wasn't big or new or equipped with every comfort, but she was safe and fairly reliable. And she was something more. She was a means of reaching people who couldn't be reached any other way.

Traveling on the *Kuto Misa,* we were able to complete a health survey of the people along the river. We knew we couldn't treat many diseases without costly equipment and hospitals, but we thought we could do something about a problem common to all the villages along the river—river blindness.

Almost all of the population was infected with onchocerciasis (commonly called river blindness), a disease caused by a parasitic worm that is transmitted by the bite of the black fly that breeds along rivers. When the worms infect the eye, it causes scar tissue resulting in permanent blindness. It could be controlled inexpensively with the drug ivermectin, if only the villagers had access to the drug.

Talking it over after our trip, we knew we couldn't just walk away from the situation once we'd seen it. We had a boat. We had three local staff members in Omba, Papa Akula, and Shamba. They were willing to deliver the river blindness drug, vitamins, immunizations, and other basic health needs; the rest of us were confident that we could raise the money for the program. That's how we started Rivers of the World (ROW), an exploration and international development organization. Our mission has always been to work with people in remote areas to help them solve their problems.

Since that first trip, ROW has continued to grow beyond our wildest imaginations. Last year, our team treated more than 200,000 people for river blindness, despite a war in the Congo. With the backing of his church, Dr. Chris Price and ROW volunteers revived the hospital in Lus-ambo and filled it with $250,000 worth of medicines. We're raising money for a floating clinic to travel the Napo River basin in Peru and fighting malaria in South America.

ROW teams have built libraries and run dental clinics in Belize. Andrae Crouch wrote and recorded a song for us, and others donated their music for a fundraising CD. We have broadcast educational and inspirational programs from Peru, the Congo, and all over the world. American students raise money for river blindness and people donate their talents to create t-shirts and audiotapes, whose sale brings in more money to travel more rivers and help more people.

ROW is living proof that a handful of people, even one person, can make a difference in the world. All you need is a dream, and well, maybe a boat. As you've just read, it doesn't take a luxury cruiser. Sometimes just grabbing the first coffee barge that comes along will get the job done. The important thing is to get on board.

About the Author

Ben Mathes is the president of Rivers of the World (**www.row.org**), an international exploration and development agency. In addition, he is the author of the audio book and DVD series, entitled *Lessons From the Forests*. Learn more at **www. lessonsfromtheforests.com**.

Laura Raines is a freelance writer. She lives in Atlanta, Georgia, with her husband, Greg, and her two daughters, Sarah and Frances; and she travels vicariously with Rivers of the World.

0-595-23436-4